The Guru's Gift

The Guru's Gift

*An Ethnography
Exploring Gender Equality with
North American Sikh Women*

CYNTHIA MAHMOOD
University of Maine

STACY BRADY

Mayfield Publishing Company
Mountain View, California
London • Toronto

Library of Congress Cataloging-in-Publication Data
Mahmood, Cynthia Keppley.
    The Guru's gift : an ethnography exploring gender equality with North American Sikh women / Cynthia Mahmood, Stacy Brady.
        p.   cm.
    Includes bibliographical references and index.
    ISBN 0-7674-1781-x
    1. Women—Religious aspects—Sikhism.   2. Feminism—Religious aspects—Sikhism.   3. Sikh women—Religious life—North America.   4. Equality—North America.   5. Sex role—North America.   I. Brady, Stacy.   II. Title.

BL2018.5.W65 M34 1999
305.48'6946073—dc21

                                                                    99-047704

Manufactured in the United States of America
10   9   8   7   6   5   4   3   2

Mayfield Publishing Company
1280 Villa Street
Mountain View, CA 94041

Sponsoring editor, Janet M. Beatty; production editor, Deneen Sedlack; manuscript editor, Margaret Moore; art and design manager, Susan Breitbard; text and cover designer, Anne Flanagan; cover photo by Rubin Paul Singh; manufacturing manager, Randy Hurst. The text was set in 10/12.5 Palatino by TBH Typecast, Inc. and printed on acid-free 50# Finch Opaque by Malloy Lithographing, Inc.

Text Credits: Chapter 2, p. 26 Copyright © 1995 by Nikky Gurinder Kaur Singh. Singh, Nikky Gurinder Kaur. *The Name of My Beloved* pp. 52–53. San Francisco: Harper. Reprinted by permission of the author. Chapter 3, p. 77 Copyright © 1980 by The University of Massachusetts Press. First appeared in *Two-Headed Woman,* published by The University of Massachusetts Press. Now appears in *Good Woman: Poems and a Memoir 1969–1980,* published by BOA Editions, Ltd. Copyright © 1987 by Lucille Clifton. Reprinted by permission of Curtis Brown, Ltd. Chapter 4, p. 78 Matrimonial advertisement from www.SikhNet.com. Reprinted by permission of the author.

Photo Credits: Chapter 3, p. 62, Figure 3.1; Courtesy of Sikh Heritage Calendar. Chapter 3, p. 74, Figure 3.2; Courtesy of Dina Goldstein. Chapter 2, p. 37, Figure 2.1; Chapter 4, p. 86, Figure 4.1; Chapter 5, p. 108, Figure 5.1; Chapter 5, p. 111, Figure 5.2; Courtesy of Cynthia Mahmood and Stacy Brady.

Preface

This book is an experiment in feminist ethnographic research, decentering the role of the scholar/author in favor of a more respectful inclusion of the voices of those we are attempting to understand. North American women who have chosen Sikhism as a faith path (and it will become clear that this is very much a conscious choice, not unthinking tradition) are perfectly capable of speaking for themselves, and do so volubly, fluently, and with determination. We give them a forum in which to speak through this publication, offering our own interlocution, commentaries, translations, and criticisms in the spirit of sisterhood. These Sikh women challenged and inspired us, and we invite you to share in our provocative journey into the world of women who are rethinking, remolding, and reinvigorating transnational Punjabi culture and the Sikh religious tradition today.

Just as we prefer not to distance ourselves from our "subjects" but to embrace them in their full humanity, as feminists we also reject the distancing that has classically permeated relations between teachers and students. This book is therefore an experiment in pedagogy as well. Stacy Brady is an undergraduate student, and Cynthia Mahmood is an associate professor. Consciously combating the hierarchies that shape the traditional North American learning environment, we choose to relate to each other as senior and junior colleagues rather than as authoritative professor and assimilative pupil. Clearly, one of us is further along in her career and life path than the other. But youth and newness can mean not only naïveté but also freshness, a lack of contamination by the vast array of assumptions that frame the academic study of religious communities.

The Sikh women who participated in this project live in several cities across the United States and Canada. We choose to use pseudonyms in this book and to protect the identities of those who worked with us by occasionally altering a detail such as a place name or other identifying information. Some of these women are already vocal activists in their communities and are well known, but others choose a lower profile and may have much to lose if publicly marked as "feminist" due to their appearance in this book. The women who appear in the photographs accompanying this text have consented to appear here and are *not* the women interviewed.

Innovations in writing go right along with innovations in collaborative styles of research. We thought extensively about how to preserve "voice" in this book without relinquishing cohesion; we thought about what coauthorship means in a situation in which one of us is a professor and the other a student. In the end, we opted for an eclectic mix. We hope that readers find our conversation here, on which they are invited to eavesdrop, to be of help as they engage in their own conversations about women, faith, culture, and power.

Cynthia's name is listed first on the cover of this book because it is more likely to be recognized by potential readers. We consider our authorship in every way coequal and complementary, and take responsibility together for the information and opinions offered in this book.

The main readership of this book is likely to consist of non-Sikh students at North American universities. We therefore explain Punjabi terms as we use them and assume little knowledge of Sikhism or the Sikh community. Clearly, however, this book will be of some interest to Sikhs as well. We hope that it might be used as a stimulus for discussion as that community grapples with the challenges it faces in the next century. Young people growing up in the United States and Canada may be the Sikh leaders of the future; we urge that senior members of the community hear their voices and help them to fully claim the unique gift of the Sikh Gurus: equality between women and men. This book is just an exploratory effort; with the commitment of the community, a more comprehensive study of the issue of gender equality in Sikhism— the diasporan, transnational, vibrant Sikhism of today—will be possible.

At the University of Maine we thank the Women in the Curriculum and Women's Studies programs, the Canadian-American Center, the Anthropology Department, and the College of Education. We also thank Phyllis Brazee, Nikky Singh, Kristin Langellier, John Sherblom, Judy Redding, and I. J. Singh. We'd also like to thank the two reviewers of the manuscript for their incisive comments: Amrita Basu, Amherst College, and Martha C. Ward, University of New Orleans. Any mistakes in the book are entirely our own, however.

We thank all the people at Mayfield, especially Jan Beatty, who took a chance with our experiment in ethnographic research and writing.

Most of all we thank the Sikh women we now know and love as friends, for their grace, their eloquence, and their courage.

We thank Khalid and Matt, the men in our lives, and Naintara and Chelsea, our little women.

Orono, Maine
July 1999

Contents

1

Women's Lives

Stacy Brady's Story

This project began in 1995 while I was an education major who had joined the honors program at the University of Maine looking for a little challenge. I went to a luncheon lecture in the spring given by Dr. Cynthia Mahmood on the topic of "Women Refugees and Gender in Asylum Law." As a student in Cynthia's anthropology classes, I had heard about her work with Sikh militants in the United States and Canada, but I was particularly curious about how the women fared in a situation of armed conflict like that involving the Sikhs of Punjab. There must be women Sikh refugees: Why do we never hear about them? Cynthia gave examples of how many Sikh women in Punjab had been the victims of horrendous violence perpetrated by both sides of the conflict and how, if they were lucky enough to make it to the United States or Canada, they often were subjected to culturally inappropriate and humiliating procedures in order to secure safe refuge for themselves and their children. The talk stirred a sense of injustice in me, and I talked with Dr. Mahmood afterwards about what could be done to correct the situation and to educate public officials about the culture and background of the women with whom they were dealing. In short, I wanted to know what I could do to help.

In Cynthia's office, we talked about the need for a better understanding of minority populations in North America, like the Sikhs, and the political and social assumptions that frame immigration laws and refugee decisions. It became clear to me that I had no understanding of the complexity or diversity of Sikh communities in North America and that to hope that I could offer even the smallest assistance, I needed to learn more about the people, culture, religion, and politics—both of the transmigrant or diasporan Sikh community in North America and of their homeland in the state of Punjab, India. It so happened that just at that time Cynthia was trying to arrange a trip to a Massachusetts *gurudwara*, or house of worship, for students interested in learning more about her work and Sikhism in general. I signed up for the field trip, not knowing quite what to expect.

At the time of my initiation into the world of the Sikhs, I was a "nontraditional" or older undergraduate student (late twenties), who had made the decision to major in education and to plan for a career in elementary school teaching but had become sidetracked by a fascination with anthropology. As I moved on to double-major in education and anthropology, I became aware that this pattern was not uncommon. There were only a small number of students who knew from the outset that they wanted to study anthropology. More were attracted to this field by a course or an instructor or an exotic culture whose intrigues could not be pieced out in just a semester-long course. For many of us, the curiosity to find out more about cultural diversity became a thirst for knowledge that never seemed satiated. We kept taking course after course, still not committed to choosing long-term careers in anthropology but persisting in the quest to find out how humans like ourselves, in so many diverse circumstances, constructed meaning in their lives, established relationships with one another, and interpreted their place in the universe.

Many anthropologists believe that fieldwork, the on-the-ground, face-to-face study of culture, is the best form of anthropological education. The weekend field trip to the Sikh *gurudwara* outside of Boston certainly convinced me of that. In the van on the way southward from Maine, we students chattered and speculated about what awaited us in this alien place of worship. We were nervous but excited: Would anyone talk to us? Would we attract a lot of attention? Would we remember the basic rules of behavior Cynthia had laid out for us? As a person of faith myself, I kept in mind the basic idea that the Sikhs, too, were believers, that we would be praying and worshiping with them, and that this created a commonality between us despite our many differences of culture.

It was a rainy evening when we arrived, and we students dashed one by one from the van to the front entrance to the *gurudwara*. On entering, I remember a room with bright red carpet, no chairs, and Christmas lights strung high along the clean white walls. There was a kind of throne or altar at the front, on which I knew that the Sikh holy book, the Guru Granth Sahib, was ensconced. Shoes off and head covered, I walked up to the holy book and knelt before it, touching my head to the ground as a gesture of respect. I was terrified that my head covering would slip off, which I knew would be a faux pas, and I tried to inconspicuously hold it on with one hand as I bowed down. (For Sikh women it is second nature to keep these head coverings on, but for most outsiders it is a matter of conscious effort.) As I watched the other students repeat the process of bowing in front of the Guru Granth Sahib, I realized that this house of worship was not much different from the many others I had visited; churches and synagogues, mosques and meetinghouses have a certain feel to them, and this was no different. It was a place where people communed with God.

After we prayed briefly with the *granthi,* or scripture-reader, we were ushered downstairs for a late dinner prepared by a group of visibly tired but hospitable younger women. They were sisters, daughters of the *granthi,* and pharmacists. They were called in to feed us when the *granthi* realized we hadn't eaten and it was almost midnight. They needed to be up and out to work by six the next morning so they didn't stay long. We talked for only ten minutes, but this brief encounter sparked the interest in Sikh women that led me to work with Cynthia to research and write this book.

The three sisters were wearing the elegant yet functional tunic-and-pants suits common among Punjabis, and they were friendly, but quiet, as they talked with us in the hallway of the *gurudwara.* I plied Cynthia with questions after our too-brief encounter. Why do some women wear turbans while others do not? Can a woman become a *granthi?* What about arranged marriages? As we set up our sleeping bags on the clean expanse of carpet in the main hall, we talked about these women and what their lives must be like. Cynthia confessed how little she, too, knew about Sikh women; her work thus far had focused on militants of the movement to establish a Sikh state of Khalistan, and they were mostly male. I was intrigued, and fell into a fitful sleep.

To make a long story short, I began to consider making research on Sikh women a major topic of my undergraduate honors thesis. I wondered whether, as a novice in the field of Sikh studies, I could dare to approach members of the Sikh community with all of my questions about women and their roles. But by perusing the literature, it became clear how meager the written resources really were on the women of this community. Somebody should look into this, Cynthia said, and she encouraged me to think that we could do it together.

My first dose of "fieldwork" was in a Canadian city, where Cynthia had arranged that I stay with a Sikh family. She was staying nearby, and I was to phone each day with reports of what I was doing. What an adventure! On the plane my hands were trembling as we touched down—even though this was not New Guinea but nearby Canada. I knew how important the initiatory experience of field research was to a potential anthropologist, wherever the location and however exotic or familiar the culture. And I knew how much trust Cynthia put in me to treat my Sikh hosts respectfully and with all the warmth she herself feels for them.

As I traveled to other cities in the United States and Canada doing the research that led to this book, I found that there was little need to worry as I did that first night at the Boston *gurudwara* or on the airplane as we landed at our first field site. Over and over again, I have been welcomed warmly into Sikh homes, places of worship, and community gatherings. I formed friendships with many of the women I came to know. So today, when I hear outsiders comment that the Sikh community is an insular, exotic, and narrowly fundamentalist population, I feel oddly disturbed. As I was introduced to this community by an already welcomed and respected scholar, Cynthia Mahmood, I never felt other than totally accepted. It has been a privilege to come to know the people I studied and learned from, and my own life will never be the same after this deeply provocative encounter. I'm still uneasy about whether what I did was really "ethnography," but I do know that it was the experience of a lifetime.

Like many students in the '90s, I didn't have what one might label a classical education in anthropology. I started out by reading not the traditional ethnographies and analyses by anthropological giants like Radcliffe-Brown, Malinowski, or even Margaret Mead, but instead began with a steady literary diet of what some have termed "experimental" ethnographies (Marcus and Fischer 1986). The term "experimental" can be read as "feminist" or "humanist," as if these ethnographies were illegitimate children of the proud "scientific" discipline of anthropology. I read life histories like *Nisa,* by Marjorie Shostak (1981) and *Aman,* coauthored by Aman, Virginia Lee Barnes, and Janice Boddy (1994). I read Nancy Scheper-Hughes' *Death Without Weeping* (1992), Phillippe Bourgois' *In Search of Respect* (1995), and, of course, Cynthia Mahmood's *Fighting for Faith and Nation* (1996). I admired the way these researchers had been able to build bridges between their interlocutors' world views and experiences and how they always convey the common humanity underlying very diverse ways of life. I began to think that all ethnographies were written in this manner; these were not "experimental" to me but they seemed a perfectly natural way of writing and reflecting on how people around the world lived their lives.

It was only later on that I realized these books represented only a relatively recent and controversial trend in the discipline. In older, more traditional ethnographies, the researcher was not "present" in the text and the subjects of the research were themselves barely present, often physically described but stripped of the things that made them real and tangible as human beings. There was also a difference in the attitude or ethics of the researcher. The books I was drawn to were written by people who saw themselves as intimately tied in one way or another to the people they researched. There was a distinctly activist stance taken by many of these authors that resonated with my own initial attraction to the Sikh community—that is, that many North American Sikhs came here as refugees from conflict in Punjab. These types of ethnographies are commonly criticized as being too close to the subjects and therefore a suspiciously subjective (and therefore scientifically invalid) form of research, but I found them the most honest, realistic, and inspiring of the books I read in the field of anthropology. I had read Carrithers' article, "Is Anthropology Art or Science?" (1990) and the debate on anthropological activism by Scheper-Hughes (1995) and D'Andrade (1995), but I had little idea how concrete these issues would become as I engaged in my own research and writing.

I wrestled with debates about science and humanism in anthropology before we left for "the field" in order to clarify how my own relationships with the Sikhs would begin to take shape. Did I want to maintain a distant observer stance and then jump into the ethnographic moment to prove I was there, to establish "authority" as an analyst of Sikh culture, as James Clifford (1983) puts it? Feminist theory and methods, to which I had also been extensively exposed, cautioned me to examine how different structures of texts and ethnographic writings can hide or convey power relationships between the researcher and the researched. How would my own positionality (Harding 1991) as a white woman of middle-class background affect the research among women of color and possibly very different backgrounds and experiences? Trinh Min-ha suggests radically, in her classic *Woman Native Other* (1989), that any investigation into "others" is pervaded by projections, constructions, and oppositions of the self—particularly insidious where unequal power relations hold sway. Chilla Bulbeck, another feminist scholar, recommends a way around this by starting with the familiar and increasingly enlarging its boundaries when women of dominant cultures seek to work with women who may differ in the positions of power in race or class (1998). As it turned out, many of the women with whom we worked were women of my own age group and class level who had similar or more extensive education than myself. We differed mostly on the race axis and, of course, resulting life experiences, but in the end this research was relatively level in terms of power relations and avoided some (but not all) of the typical "top-down" power issues. But my feminist awareness of power issues remained a subtext of every conversation I had with Sikh women and of every line I wrote about them.

It was additionally necessary to reflect over the recently amended ethical code for the American Anthropological Association (1998) to determine what my responsibilities were as a researcher. I found that I kept coming back to one particular phrase that already had intrinsic meaning for me—"covenantal relationship." The concept of covenantal relationship is defined in this new ethical code as a close and enduring relationship that operates under openness and informed consent and with mutually beneficial research and shared objectives. The concept of a covenant with the people one studies formed the cornerstone of my approach to Sikh women, who were not merely "subjects" of research but who became friends and (fictive) sisters. This kind of bond does not dissolve on completion of an academic project or achievement of an academic publication, but is a continuing relationship and mutual obligation. I could relate to this through my understanding of the "covenant" between a minister and her or his congregation; it is not just a *job* that we are talking about here.

It was through interactions between Sikh women and myself that the parameters of this project were set up and joint goals established. In addition to myself and the women with whom I worked, however, there was the continuing physical, emotional, intellectual, and political presence of my teacher, Cynthia Mahmood. Her life and mine intertwined as both of us became entangled with women of the North American Sikh community. We are student and teacher, protégée and mentor, junior and senior colleagues, and friends. So our dialogue informs at every point what we think and write about the women we study.

We claim nothing more than this for the book you are holding in your hands: that it tells the tale of some fascinating and inspiring young women of a faith tradition most outside that community don't know much about, and that it represents how education-as-apprenticeship can work and work well. We invite students and educators, Sikh women and Sikh men, to join us in our continuing exploration.

Cynthia Mahmood's View

The period when Stacy Brady and I were getting to know each other was the time immediately following the publication of my book on Sikh separatism, *Fighting for Faith and Nation*. (I had seen her as one of some five hundred faces in my intro-to-anth lectures, but that doesn't entirely count!) When Stacy began to take upper-level classes in anthropology and to make herself known to me as an individual, it was a time of some distress for me. The reason for the distress—indeed, depression—was that after my book came out I didn't hear much from the Sikh community about it, even from those Sikhs who had worked directly with me on the project, with whom I had shared deeply intense encounters surrounding their narratives of violence and war. Having eaten, slept, and breathed militant Sikhism for the past four years or so, this sudden denouement felt traumatic. More than that, it felt lonely. Had my interest in them been totally nonreciprocal? Did they, in fact, hate what I had written about them?

In deepening frustration, I talked with a colleague about these feelings, which I had not expected.

"I don't see why you are surprised," he said. "Of course ethnography is nonreciprocal. They may be central to *your* life, but you're not much part of theirs at all. And furthermore," he added, "it should be that way."

As our conversation proceeded, my colleague (also a friend) reassured me on what he perhaps thought was my perception that my book was no good. "Look," he said, "you managed to get closer to these people than anybody else has. That's a real achievement, and you should be proud of yourself for it."

I nodded, but as I heard those well-meant words I realized that my understanding of ethnography was radically different from his. I didn't view the Sikh militants in terms of an *accomplishment* but, rather, in terms of a set of ongoing relationships. These relationships were and are, of course, constrained in many important ways. But yes, however naive it may sound, I did expect—and desire—a certain reciprocity, a certain mutuality of respect, affection, and interest, in the ethnographic enterprise. If they, in fact, objected to my book, that was one thing, but I wanted then to hear about it, from them, directly. My book was done, but I didn't feel like my involvement with the Sikh community was "done," or ever could be.

So when Stacy Brady began to show a serious interest in further research with the Sikhs, I thought, why not? Indeed, in my work with militants I had been increasingly pegged into a sort of "one of the guys" niche; I hung out in the mostly male political environment, my attempts at entering kitchens in the spirit of sisterly solidarity gently rebuffed. I had interviewed one woman militant, and a few women who had been victims of government-sponsored atrocities, but I knew well how much more was there to be explored. The academic literature on Sikh women is minimal; there was work here to be done.

Doing fieldwork with students is one of the great joys of being a teacher of anthropology. It is so enormously more productive than any amount of classroom learning. But it does open one to certain kinds of risks in terms of the authority and respect we professors are used to getting within the ivy-covered walls of our universities. In this case, I realized I was making myself highly vulnerable to Stacy; our first field trip to find Sikh women to interview was also the first time I was returning to a Sikh environment after the publication of my book. I was to speak at a major dinner at the Canadian Parliament involving important members of the Sikh community. Were they going to reject me and my book? Stacy would be there to see the whole thing. At that point I wasn't even sure whether all my vaunted "contacts" in that community, which could presumably help her to find women to talk with, were still my contacts to pass on.

We talked about this situation, and we talked about what a more reciprocal ethnography, as I was coming to conceptualize it, would be like. Stacy was a double major in education and anthropology, and we talked a lot about pedagogical strategies and these issues of authority and vulnerability and what they meant. In the end, we thought that we could trust each other with our mutual vulnerabilities (Stacy: Could she do "ethnography"? Would the Sikh women actually be willing to talk with her? Me: Were the Sikhs going to reject me? Had they in fact forgotten entirely about me after the militancy research was "done"?), and we embarked together on the journey that led to this book.

Stacy did ethnography and she did it well; Sikh women not only talked with her but also expressed their most deeply held beliefs and values and shared their most intimate experiences. The Sikhs did not reject me (though some did criticize my book!), and it became wonderfully clear to me that they also viewed my relationship with them as ongoing and mutual. This is not to say that any part of this project was easy. It was not. Now both of us have ongoing relationships with Sikhs, and these relationships continue to be fraught with ethical and other kinds of dilemmas. But our "field" is not some location away from our own lives; it's here all around us, entwined with who we are. We think that's how it should be.

Although we began this project in the context of independent study and thesis research in anthropology, it became clear that any text that would emerge from this would have a substantial women's studies interest. We hadn't expected to find the Sikh women with whom we talked so involved with their own empowerment and so courageous in thinking that through in terms of their own religious tradition. Living in the context of an ongoing women's movement in North America, these women nevertheless seek their equality not through Canadian or American feminism but through Sikhism —and not as an innovation within Sikhism but as a reclamation of something they perceive as already there. As Western feminism extends its vision to every corner of the globe, the interpretation of women's issues within highly diverse cultural contexts has become an important issue. What shall we make of Islamic women who *choose* to veil rather than rebelling against veiling, of women who celebrate homemaking and childrearing as natural niches for their gender, who prefer that their parents choose their spouses rather than relying on the vagaries of "love"? We thought that these Sikh women, who speak in the same idiom as that of most of our probable readers but have very different ideas of what gender equality means, could give us insight into these areas.

Furthermore, as our own collaboration in anthropology proceeded, we realized that it actually echoed a great deal of theory about feminist education and how it should work. This wasn't really conscious planning on our part. But when students and teachers relate to each other on a simple human-to-human level, what you get ends up looking a lot like feminist pedagogy. Similarly, when anthropologists drop some of their pretensions to special knowledge and treat the people they study as coexplorers, they end up writing tracts some call feminist ethnographies—for example, Ruth Behar and Esperanza in *Translated Woman* (1993), whose relationship is as central as the "information" (or worse, "data") presented in the book, and Lila Abu-Lughod's Bedouin "informants" (or worse, "subjects"), whose life crises mirrored, echoed, and intertwined with her own in *Writing Women's Worlds* (1993). All forms of scholarship in the social studies are benefiting from these humanistic impulses today.

Edith Turner, who was an "anthropological wife" in the field with Victor Turner when he was doing his famous research on Ndembu in the 1950s, later emerged with her own quite different take on the process of ethnography. She dared to write of "advocacy anthropology in the female style, that is, speaking on behalf of a culture as a lover or a mother" (1987:x). We follow Edie, with great respect and admiration, in imagining ethnographic bonds as covenantal, as obligational, and as permeated by love. It wasn't easy for her to say this when she did, and, in many academic environments, it's still not easy. If yours is one of those, perhaps this book will help.

Now Stacy introduces, in her own voice, the initial set of women who participated in this project—who are now our friends—and whose words are recorded in the thematic chapters that follow. Other women would join in later and, eventually, some men as well. But the first group of participants in our research were young women Stacy met during research for her thesis. Little did she, or they, imagine they would all end up being read in college classes, that their words would find a home in university libraries.

Surjeet Kaur[1]

I met Surjeet at a Sikh youth retreat, and she agreed to be my very first interviewee. She was a twenty-year-old university student and lived at home with her parents and her younger sister. Many of the girls at the retreat were dressed in Punjabi clothes, some with turbans, but Surjeet wore her hair long and seemed very comfortable in her T-shirt and sweatpants. She struck me as immediately friendly and eager to hear about and participate in our research. I lost my nervousness quickly as I realized that Surjeet was just like any number of the students I sat next to in university classes. It was because I was caught up in the idea of being an "anthropologist" with an "informant" that I was feeling some trepidation. I decided to get my mind outside

---

[1] All names used in this book are fictitious. Note that Sikh women have the surname "Kaur," meaning princess, and Sikh men have the surname "Singh," meaning lion, in accordance with Sikh tradition.

of that framework and just get to know Surjeet, as one young woman to another.

We decided to go canoeing with a group of women at the retreat, so we all headed down to the boat dock to get our life preservers and our boats. It was a cloudless summer day, and Surjeet and I talked as we attempted to maneuver our canoe around the lake, chatting about where we were from and our respective backgrounds. Most of the others had gone in after a half hour or so, but Surjeet and I enjoyed ourselves just drifting around and talking until we both noticed something move in the water about ten feet away from us. At first it looked like a turtle taking a look around, but then there was a distinctive undulating movement coming from the area. We both grabbed our paddles and started back to shore as fast as we could. We discovered we had something else in common: a visceral fear of snakes! Canoeing, snakes—no "ethnography" so far. But I felt at home, in my own skin, not in the costume-like pretension of being a "scholar."

Surjeet led me back to the now-empty dining hall where we had eaten earlier in the day, and we got comfortable on the floor while I turned my tape recorder on. By then, we felt free enough with each other that the recorder did not seem to intrude too much. Surjeet talked about her decision to live at home while she went to school and how it was the best for everyone involved:

> I wasn't ready to leave at eighteen years old. I was very emotionally dependent on my family, even though I tried to prove otherwise. I was like "Oh, I don't need you! I am mature enough and I can do whatever I want!" But when it came down to it, I wasn't at a point in my life where I would be able to juggle the responsibility of doing well in school and the new lifestyle of being on my own.

I asked Surjeet if she thought that being "emotionally dependent" on her family was a bad thing and if it was typical for daughters, as opposed to sons, to live at home while going to college. She responded,

> For someone who is eighteen years old, being emotionally dependent is not necessarily a bad thing [laughs]. I guess it is good. It makes my parents happy. They have got me for a couple more years at least [laughs again]. . . . As far as daughters or sons living at home, it really varies and it depends on the family and the upbringing of the parents.

This is a sample of the sort of "interviews" I conducted, more of which appear in later chapters. Let me move on to briefly introduce the other women with whom I talked.

Sukhminder Kaur

A different city. My hosts had arranged for us to go to sightseeing for the day, and the plan was that when we got back there would be women there for me to meet and maybe interview. We had a lovely day but had run into a significant amount of traffic both going to and coming from the different tourist sights in the area because it was a national holiday. We were running about two hours late by the time we got close to their neighborhood, and I asked Mr. Singh, a contact of Cynthia Mahmood's who was helping me out, if the women would be angry that they had been kept waiting so long. Mr. Singh said teasingly, "You will get to see firsthand the bravery of the Sikh women! Right now, they are waiting for you with sticks. I am going to be sure to tell them that you are the reason why we were so late!" At that point, it wasn't their bravery I was worried about. This was one of the things about fieldwork that was hardest for me to deal with: the lack of control. You have to be willing to relinquish a lot of autonomy, to put yourself in others' hands sometimes.

When we got to the house, I jumped out of the car and dashed upstairs for my tape recorder and notes and ran back downstairs where I was greeted by three young women. Sukhminder, twenty, introduced herself and her friend Harinder as students from the local university and as members of the Sikh students' association on campus and were accompanied by Harmanjot. We all decided to do separate interviews, but agreed that everyone could stay if they wished and provide feedback during the conversations.

Sukhminder exuded confidence and, although she had decided she was not ready for the commitment necessary to become "baptized" as an orthodox Sikh, she felt very strongly about the merits of her faith. As we talked about Sukhminder's views on Sikhism and its influences on her life, she recalled how at one time she had doubted the existence of God completely:

> Growing up, my parents never really said, "This is our religion, you have to sit there, you have to go to Sikhism class and Punjabi class every week." My parents were very busy people and they have always been busy, so I never really had the experience of somebody teaching me the religion. Then I took this philosophy course in high school and it really opened my eyes because I realized I didn't know if there was a God. So I was sitting on this fence—there is no proof that there is no God and there is no proof that there is a God. I was sitting right in the middle.
>
> Then I took this Sikhism class in college, thinking "This is going to be easy, I'll go to class once in a while and it will be no problem!" I actually found myself wanting to go to the lectures because it was so interesting. I found that the way that Guru Nanak [the first teacher of Sikhism] explained God was just phenomenal, because

there is no attempt at physical description. God is really beyond our understanding, though we can try to live in tune with divine spirit. That's the way to comprehend what religious belief is. It is a way of living.

Sikhism is such a modern religion and it can fit so well with our day-to-day lives. There are no strict rules and regulations as to what is supposed to happen. It is a faith of the common people, and it is so simple. That is the beauty of it. God is everywhere and God is nowhere. And God has no gender and no form, shapeless, you know? I think this is very interesting because we all grow up as little children thinking that there is a man up there deciding what to do and what not to do.

Sukhminder talked further about her love for Punjabi culture and dancing but expressed her frustration that some people in the Sikh community confused cultural values or traditions with Sikhism's religious principles:

I am into the culture big time and some people have come to me and said, "You dance and dancing is wrong. A Sikh girl should not be dancing!" I am totally against this. I will do what I want to do and no one is going to be able to come to me and say I am wrong for doing this because in Sikhism everything is out in the open and that is important to me. Show me where dancing is something that goes against the divine spirit.

I was starting to realize that these young women not only were thoughtful but also could be quite eloquent about their ideas. The transcripts would not need much editing. Indeed, I suspected that these women could just as well write their own book! But Cynthia reassured me that the role of a broker or translator of sorts, of a provider of context, was also a useful one.

Learning about the Sikh faith also stimulated me to think about my own beliefs and my own spiritual path: *reflexivity*, as it is called in anthropology—welcoming the challenges to one's own world view that arise in the ethnographic encounter.

Harinder Kaur

When we finished the first interview with Sukhminder, we took some time to sip hot *chai* (Indian tea) and snack on some fresh fruit and homemade cookies that my hosts brought in to keep us going. We talked about what our goals for the research were and how these women felt that often non-Sikhs did not do a very good job trying to understand or explain the complex relationship between Punjabi immigrant culture and the current practices and beliefs that represent Sikhism among the younger generation.

Harinder was twenty-one and a second-generation Canadian Sikh. She and Sukhminder were active in cultural and religious activities of Sikh students on their college campus. She has the goal of getting her MBA someday and feels that she is really fortunate to have her family's support for her education:

> I think that getting an education is one of the biggest things with Sikhs, as long as the parents are educated. Usually the preferences are for the kids to become a doctor or a lawyer or something like that. Because the parents came here [to North America] for you, the children. They had their education back home, and they gave all of that up for you. I feel that we owe them something for this. The Sikh community is so very often willing to pay to make sure its younger people are educated. My dad, if it has anything to do with academics, he will pay for it. A lot of people are very lucky that way, especially in this day and age. I have never had a problem in school or with anything I wanted, as long as I studied and worked hard and I think that is a good agreement.[2]

Like her friend Sukhminder, Harinder felt that she was not ready yet to take *amrit* (to become initiated as an orthodox Sikh). Her parents had taken it when she was a child, but she said at that point she had never really understood the significance of their decision. She describes her own faith journey as a process of "slowly educating myself" and could picture herself taking *amrit* later on down the road "possibly after marriage but not before."

Harmanjot Kaur

Harmanjot had the patience of a saint. She was the third woman waiting for me with Sukhminder and Harinder, but she had been waiting almost two hours for me while the other women had heard I was running late and so had delayed coming over until just before I arrived. Harmanjot accepted my apologies with grace and was still enthusiastic to talk with me.

Harmanjot was twenty-eight and had been married one year. She was the first turbaned Sikh woman I interviewed, and yet it did not occur to me at the time to ask her about her decision to wear a turban (usually worn by Sikh men). Later, of course, I wished I had taken the time to ask her about it. The only reference she made to it while we were talking was that after

---

[2] As a matter of fact, it is not only educated Sikhs who prioritize education for their children; the entire Sikh community in North America is characterized by a parental emphasis on schooling.

she had taken *amrit* four years ago, the only major change that she had made was to keep her hair long as mandated in the Sikh faith and to cover her head.

Harmanjot was born in England and was raised by her grandparents because her father was in the army and he traveled a lot. She never mentioned what had happened to her mother. She said that in her home growing up, the girls in the family were treated the same as or sometimes better than her only brother:

> The girls are more educated. I have only one brother and he is on his own. The girls were on their own too. We all worked for ourselves. We had jobs and then we went to university.
>
> My brother did the same thing, he was treated no different. Actually, I think he was treated more poorly than the rest of us [laughs]!"

After Harmanjot's interview was finished, Sukhminder and Harinder said their good-byes and Harmanjot and I were called in to have our dinner while her husband and other young Sikh men talked in the living room with Mr. Singh. It was nice to have the chance to turn the tape recorder off and just share a meal together, although I was feeling increasingly comfortable with the joint ethnographer-cum-friendly-acquaintance role. Over warm *chappatis* (flat breads) and a delicious meal of basmati rice, lentils, and a fiery chickpea stew, Harmanjot and I talked about her job at a local communications company, her psychology degree, and her aspirations of teaching at the college level someday. We also traded stories about being married, our husbands, and her recent trip to visit her husband's family in Punjab. I was glad that these women were interested in me, too, and I was ready to share myself with them as much as they were ready to share with me.

Amanpreet Kaur

One of the young men, Jarnail, who introduced himself at a Sikh youth retreat I attended, said that he thought it would be great for me to meet his friend Amanpreet and her husband who lived in the area. He asked if I would mind if he arranged for me to stay with them for a few days while I was there and said they could introduce me to other women they knew. This was an especially good stroke of luck for me because, otherwise, I might not have had the chance to meet one of the people who came to shape the focus of this research the most.

I had received gifts of several beautiful Punjabi suits while I stayed with my hosts, Gurdip Singh and his extended family, and they took an obvious delight in seeing me walking down the stairs in them each morning. (Punjabi women typically wear a long tunic, loose pants, and a matching scarf.) As I waited for Amanpreet to pick me up to take me to their house for a few nights, I took pictures and played with the six children. They were doing a great job with a poor student anthropologist who was trying to learn the Punjabi alphabet when Amanpreet, her husband Hardev, and their friend Jarnail arrived to take me out to dinner. I am sure that we made quite a picture as we walked into the Italian restaurant: a blonde in a Punjabi suit and three turbaned Canadian Sikhs in jeans and polo shirts!

Amanpreet had a soft voice, but a sharp sense of humor. We laughed a lot over dinner and seemed to hit it off right away. They explained they had decided to take me to an Italian restaurant because they guessed I could use a break from Indian cuisine for one night. Amanpreet and Jarnail worked as computer analysts for companies in the area, and Hardev worked in technology research. They had many ideas of different people they knew who would be good to talk with and emphasized the need for me to meet women of different backgrounds. These people were so well connected throughout their community, I knew I was once again in the right hands. A lot of ethnography is serendipity, I had learned in classes, and my experience in the field certainly verified that.

After dinner, Hardev made a few phone calls trying to see who might be available for me to speak with over the next few days and then decided to go out for a run so Amanpreet and I could talk. I began by telling Amanpreet how I thought my interview questions were off the mark and that I had begun to feel frustrated. I had hoped to find out what were some of the primary issues for Sikh women instead of guessing or imposing my own issues on the research (an objection anthropologists typically have to the prepared questionnaires and surveys used in other disciplines). Many of the younger women had told me that I was confusing parts of Punjabi culture with the religion of Sikhism and the older women were confused by the language or concepts of the original questions, but no one so far from either group had suggested a more direct way of reaching what might be important.

Amanpreet, who was in her early thirties and had been raised primarily in western Canada, looked over the questions, smiled, and said,

Well, these questions are OK, but I can see why you are having some problems.

Speaking from a younger woman's perspective, these questions don't really inspire any passion in me; these are not the kinds of things that I would want to talk about or have people know about me as a Sikh woman. If you really want to get at something that will strike a chord with the kind of Sikh women that I know, ask them "Have you had to make a conscious choice to be a Sikh woman? If so, describe the process that has led you to that choice." If you start your interviews with this question, I will almost guarantee that everything else will follow.

I knew instinctively that this was a woman with clear insight into her community and her faith and that if I took this advice the conversations with other women I talked to would be richer for it. She cautioned that some women may not feel that they needed to make such a choice because it had been so much a part of their upbringing, but she felt for most women her age this question would resonate and provide an opportunity for reflection. She was right.

This is how Amanpreet answered her own question:

> I was seventeen when I made this choice. I wanted to take amrit to make a commitment to the **Guru** [God] and I went to my parents to tell them. They said that I was too young to make such an impor-tant decision, that I was still changing, and that I should wait. I had thought a lot about this, though; I would be finishing high school and moving on to a new stage of life in a year and I knew I wanted to make choices as to which way I wanted to go.
>   I remember during that three- or four-month period I had spent a lot of time with other Sikh children and I had gone to Punjabi school from a young age. I had learned from an early age that Sikhism was a progressive faith, in terms of equal rights for women and all types of people. I knew that I wasn't going to change my mind about my faith, I would just wind up learning more about it as I got older. I made that choice maybe twelve or so years ago, but in a sense I think I make that same choice every day. Every time you are faced with a decision, either you choose to stay on the path or you don't.

The notion of conscious choice, or as scholars say nowadays, of *agency*, did turn out to be very important to all the women we knew and therefore became central to our study. We would never have thought to ask the ques-tion in that way had we not been entirely open to taking the lead not from previously published academic literature but from the women themselves.

Jasjit Kaur

Later in my travels, I was introduced to Jasjit Kaur. Jasjit was in her early twenties, and as we sat in her front living room with its family pictures and portraits of historical Sikh figures, she explained that for her becoming a

Sikh was a continually transforming process. She was so interesting to speak with precisely because she felt she was in a transition period in her identity formation as a Sikh woman. She had recently graduated from university and had made the decision to take *amrit* two years earlier. Jasjit described how the taking of *amrit* was the first concrete step in her efforts to live according to the tenets of her faith:

> It was really a lifelong thing that I had always wanted. I knew in the back of my mind that I would do this someday and it was just a matter of getting there. The decisive moment came about two months beforehand and I just said, "OK, I have to do this, I am ready. This is the time and there is no turning back because if I don't do this now I will never do it." My family is religiously inclined but they won't push you, just encourage you. I think it was my roommate who really helped, though. She was the biggest help at the time because we took up this commitment at the same time. I kept it private, otherwise. None of my friends knew what was going on and I kept it to myself. Even my Sikh friends who were nonbaptized didn't know. They knew I was inclined that way and that I would do this one day, but they didn't know it was happening so soon. I decided to tell them afterwards because if I didn't go through with it, I would feel weird about having told them.
>
> After this first step was taken, though, nothing has changed for me personally besides my religious requirements that come with being a baptized Sikh. Sometimes it is frustrating because others think that "She is different now. She can't be the same type of person she was; she can't have fun anymore." And I am always trying to tell them that I am the same human being as before. I am just trying to do something different. I am just trying to be a Sikh woman.

Jasjit was in the process of deciding whether or not she could make the commitment to wear a turban. When I spoke with her, she was wearing a large head scarf covering her hair to get used to the feeling of having something binding up her hair all the time. She told me how strongly she felt about wanting to be known and recognized as a Sikh woman as opposed to "just another South Asian immigrant." She felt that if she could make the transition from the head scarf to wearing the turban, she would have the kind of identity she wanted:

> As a Sikh woman, it is not mandatory to wear a turban. In terms of my identity, it comes down to how do I look different than anybody else? I am always confused for a Muslim woman. I want my own identity for the same reason that Sikh males wear turbans. We are always fighting that, you know? What is the Sikh identity anyway?

Karanjeet Kaur

Jasjit had two sisters who also agreed to speak with me, Karanjeet and Surpreet. Jasjit and Karanjeet were close in age and both still single while Surpreet was married and had had her first child just recently. Karanjeet had finished her undergraduate degree at the university a few years ago and was living at home with her growing extended family. Surpreet, her husband, and their baby were temporarily living with the family again until they were ready to move into their new house in the same neighborhood. When we discussed how girls and boys are typically treated in Sikh families like hers, Karanjeet felt that things could be more fair:

> There is a double standard and my mom and dad refuse to deal
> with it. My brother has been seeing someone and is now engaged,
> and this was fine with my parents. My dad had said to us [unmar-
> ried] girls, "If you were to find yourselves a nice Sikh boy, I would
> be happy with that and I would help you get married." But I know
> that would not be the case.
>   It is not that it really matters to me, about dating and marriage,
> but it is just the saddest thing how differently the girls are treated
> right from when they are born.

Karanjeet, like many others I spoke with, attributed this unequal treatment not to Sikhism but instead to Punjabi traditional culture. The value that Karanjeet cited as most important to her about her faith was the equality it embodied. She compared this to Punjabi culture, which in her eyes was very limiting for women. I asked her to explain more about this dichotomous relationship between the cultural and religious influences in her life:

> In the religion it is the equality that I value the most. It is a very free
> religion and not strict in terms of women not being allowed to do
> this or that. This is what attracted me to the religion. Punjabi cul-
> ture, however, is very traditional in terms of women. They have
> their domestic duties and stuff like that. People confuse the culture
> and the religion. They think that according to some Sikh teachings,
> their wives need to stay at home and they have to do domestic
> things. Our family has kind of been like that, but it depends more
> on the family not what the religion says. I think that as a woman,
> I would want that cleared up.

Surpreet Kaur

Surpreet, in her late twenties, was the oldest of the three sisters, had been married for three years, and was the proud mother of a beautiful baby boy.

As we talked in one part of the large family house, the rest of the family was having a wonderful time entertaining the first grandchild in the family room. I asked Surpreet if she minded having to take time away from the baby to talk, but she said that this was one of the advantages of having such a large family under one roof.

As we spoke about the influences that Sikhism has had on her life, Surpreet explained how, although she was not baptized yet, she felt she had always been "a firm Sikh." Since her marriage, however, her faith had become even stronger:

> My husband is an orthodox Sikh and he is always encouraging me in different ways, which helps to make my faith stronger. We grew up in two different countries, he in England and I in Canada, so our experiences as Sikhs have been different. His parents weren't very religious and it was he who got them involved in the religion. Then his mother got very sick, terminally ill. He was extremely close to her and he still talks about her a lot. She was bedridden for almost five years before she died, so he has seen a lot and it has made him a stronger person.
>
> When he relays those experiences to me, it makes me a stronger person too. It has helped me realize how much my religion and my family mean to me. Having faith in God has become so important to me. I used to run my life thinking I can do this or I can do that, but when you have someone close to you, like your mother, have such an illness, you realize that your life is not really in your hands. You have to rely on someone or something else at that point.
>
> You can't go through something like that completely on your own.

I realized again how important reciprocity was in these conversations, that sharing things about myself and my life was a critical part of establishing a balanced and free-flowing conversation. This was not an interrogation, after all. Observing Cynthia talking with the Sikhs, I saw that she did the same thing—as she does also in classrooms. This, too, is an inclination sometimes labeled "feminist"—not to separate public from private, one's self from one's work.

Rajvinder Kaur

Rajvinder had agreed to meet me the day after she returned from England. Although I am sure she was exhausted, she wanted to spend most of the day with me talking, having lunch, and doing some shopping in the "Little Punjab" section of the city. Rajvinder was in her mid-twenties, turbaned, and engaged to be married in three weeks in what she described as "definitely a love match." She was actively pursuing a career in law and saw herself as having more of a nontraditional marriage, in terms of being away from home a lot because of her work. We talked for hours about everything from her upcoming marriage and the plans that were being made, to her deep commitment to improving the human rights situation of the Sikhs in Punjab.

I had been asking all the women I met about their role models growing up, whether they had historical Sikh women they looked up to or if there was someone in their family who had inspired them. Rajvinder felt this was a rich topic to discuss with women her age:

> I think I was able to take characteristics of people I really respected and found that they were similar in those historic figures and my family members. I think that one thing that is definitely there is a clearly resolute sense of character.
>
> Women of my mother's generation and older have, as a group, an extremely strong ability to put others before themselves. I guess it has just been ingrained, to do things for everyone else.
>
> So it is that sense of family and sense of responsibility that I really respect. Being brought up here—to think about myself all of the time [laughs] and "what is good for me and what am I going to get out of this?"—I see these people who have spent all of their lives doing things for everybody else and I really respect that sense of sacrifice.

Later, we received a set of paintings illuminating the lives of Sikh women through history. One of them appears as an illustration in this book (Figure 3.1).

Daljot Kaur

I had met Daljot at a Sikh youth retreat, and we had arranged to meet later in the week when we both had more time to talk. I had made a classic interviewing mistake when I had agreed to meet Daljot at a local university to talk. It was a nice day and Daljot said she had been cooped up indoors all day and wanted to sit outside and enjoy some sunshine while we talked. This was fine with me except the spot she picked was directly across from a public bus stop. I thought the taped interview would be all right, but I found when I started transcribing that the bus noise would roar in my ears as I tried to hear what Daljot was saying. A very basic lesson in interview dos and don'ts: Never sit outside an airport or a bus terminal and try to tape-record an interview!

Daljot was in her early twenties, in university, and pursuing a degree in medicine. She was a baptized Sikh, turbaned, and extremely interested in Sikh politics, both in North America and in India. She talked about her experiences with the larger Indian community in her city and how there is a lot of misinformation about Sikhs and a lot of negative stereotyping:

> One day I met this Indian guy on the subway. He was sitting across from my cousin and me and he starts in on us: "Those Sikhs [in India] they are fighting and killing their own people." He was talking about the people who are fighting the police and the military. I told him that the people who they were fighting against were not their brothers, they were not really Sikhs because of what they do to innocent people. He just had this headstrong view that all Sikhs are wrong, because they are just fighting about religion. He said they didn't really have a just cause for fighting and wanting Khalistan [the separate Sikh state that is the goal of the insurgents] and they just wanted to make trouble. I think the main reason for this confusion with a lot of people like him is that there has been a lot of propaganda against Sikhs, here and in India.

Sandeep Kaur

Sandeep and I were introduced by a mutual friend. She had been asked if she could talk with me while I was in town, introduce me to some of the women she knew, and bring me to local Sikh functions where I might arrange for more interviews. Originally we met over dinner with several other people and we did not get to speak that much, but at the end of the night she handed me her phone number and said, "Call me in a day or two and we'll get together with some friends of mine." When I called back a few days later, Sandeep said there was a group she belonged to of Sikh students who got together to read and discuss scripture once a week. I jumped at the chance to attend and Sandeep agreed to pick me up and take me along as her guest.

The group was a "casual *sangat,*" or congregation, made up of Sikh university students, both men and women, who tried to interpret the Sikh scriptures for both literal language and meaning (many had trouble reading the Sikh script) and to share their own personal interpretations of the scripture's message. For me, although I couldn't understand much of the translation part of the evening, this was a very familiar and comfortable setting. My own faith journey has been largely shaped by similar gatherings of people wrestling with scripture passages and trying to express what the textual part of their faith has to say to them personally. Despite the differences in theology, the laughing, joking, and personal discussion of the group were a welcoming introduction to this particular group of friends. We sat on the floor, everyone collectively working at the translations and then each person speaking about what a particular passage had to say to her or him. After the "spiritual" part of the meeting, the group discussed their plans to serve dinner to a homeless shelter in the area (called a "kettle" project in Sikhism) and how this project would be organized.

Sandeep arranged to have me come stay with her for a night so we could talk in-depth with a few of her close friends I had met at the scripture group. Jasvinder and Taranjeet came over after they had gotten off work, bringing with them a birthday cake for Sandeep. I was deeply touched that Sandeep had forgone any other plans to have me come over on her birthday, when she could have been celebrating with these same friends. We talked and laughed over dinner and cake, then went up to Sandeep's room to continue our conversations.

Sandeep was in her early twenties and had decided to take some time off before going to graduate school. Her faith in Sikhism had had its up-and-down moments, with extremely rewarding experiences of pilgrimages to Sikh holy sites like the Harmandir Sahib in Amritsar (the "Golden Temple") to terribly destructive memories of highly political *gurudwara* fights and splits. She had spent lengthy periods of time doing service work in *gurudwaras* and villages abroad trying to learn more about what Sikhism represents as a personal faith and life commitment.

That night the three friends talked a lot about their ideas of what the "ideal" Sikh woman would be like. In a sense, they were talking about their own personal goals and aspirations using their understanding of Sikh principles as a guide. Sandeep differentiated her "ideal" from her community's collective "politically correct" stereotyped female identity:

> There is nothing wrong with a politically correct version of the ideal Sikh woman, but it is sometimes a very narrow definition. It is usually someone who is very active, doing the political work, getting involved in the political aspects of the larger Sikh community. She is very knowledgeable about both the spiritual and political aspects of the faith. She usually takes that knowledge a step further than others and decides to wear a turban. When I talk about my own personal ideas about the ideal Sikh woman, it would be more like, if you had to list some qualities about a Sikh woman that you are either aspiring to be or that you just admire, what would those qualities be? That is what I mean by ideal. Maybe ideal is not the right word to use. I think that everyone is going to have their own ideas about the characteristics or qualities that they think of when they look at Sikh women as a group.

Jasvinder Kaur

I first got to know Jasvinder through Sandeep, but we kept up our new friendship over the course of the year through e-mail. We checked in with each other periodically and had the chance to meet with each other again six months after our talk in Sandeep's bedroom. I passed along a recent paper I had finished, asking for some feedback on its accuracy and looking for things I might have missed. It was good to see her again, and she was just as friendly and sincerely interested in not just the research but also in me as a person.

Jasvinder was also in transition between school and career, trying to figure out what her next move would be. She had recently moved in again with her parents after having been away at school for quite a few years. My most recent conversation with her began with her telling me that the transition moving back under her parents' roof was harder than she had expected.

Jasvinder's family were orthodox Sikhs and had been for as long as she could remember. She described how her experience with Sikhism was different from that of many of her friends because early on her parents felt it important to teach her and her sisters about their faith and their culture. The first period of crisis in her faith came as she got older and was asked to serve on a *gurudwara* committee:

> When they first asked me, I was like "Cool! I get to be on a committee and get to be part of the decision-making process!" I was convinced I would get a lot things done that needed doing [laughing]. Once I got on the committee, that's when it all started. I saw the way that the adults behaved and treated each other. I saw the fighting and that's when it hit me—they would fight over anything! They would fight over things like construction, where to put a wall or something. Two "uncles" [fictive kin term] would just go at it, shouting at each other and saying horrible things. Every time I hear about a gurudwara fight now, I cringe because it is such a painful memory for me.
>
> Of course, I thought that if I just wrote a letter to the committee telling them to get their act together that would solve everything. Things really started going downhill for me then because the time to vote people into office was coming up again and the politics just kept getting worse. Someone had decided it was time to bring me down. I couldn't understand what I had ever done to them to deserve to be treated this way. But this all coincided with a woman running for *gurudwara* president, and the whole issue about women being in positions of power started in the *gurudwara*.

Jasvinder talked about how she has struggled through several *gurudwara* fights and how it has taken a long time for her to separate her love for

Sikhism as a religion from her disillusionment with the members of her religious institutions and her distaste for their actions.

Taranjeet Kaur

Last, but not least, I come to Taranjeet. She was also at Sandeep's that night and by far was the most outspoken of the three young women. In her mid-twenties, Taranjeet had finished her education in medicine and worked in a local clinic. She was somebody who enjoyed being outrageous and shocking, the kind of person who provoked good-natured eye-rolling from friends and openmouthed stares from more-conservative members of her community. I was at a function with her and several other young Sikhs, men and women, asking everyone for their input on subjects that I should look into for the research. I received many suggestions that I had heard before—gender equity issues, historical Sikh women and their contributions, domestic violence in the community and its causes. After everyone else had said their piece, Taranjeet spoke up and said, "You know one thing that nobody ever looks into is the homosexual component within the Sikh community. You should talk to gays and lesbians who are Sikhs." There arose a loud clamor from people at the table (mostly the men), "Oh, here she goes again! Taranjeet is always bringing lesbians into every conversation!" It was said in teasing tones, but it was a subject I knew clearly made everyone uncomfortable. There is a serious taboo for Sikhs, as in many cultures, in talking about any form of sexuality, but homosexuality is an especially distressing topic. Most religious Sikhs I have met would simply deny that it exists within their communities. I strongly suspect, despite her personal convictions, this is why Taranjeet enjoyed bringing this subject up so often. It is taboo and it makes others uncomfortable.

Later that week as we spoke about women's concerns in Sandeep's room, Taranjeet talked about how it was her understanding of Sikhism's principles that gave her the right to bring up uncomfortable or controversial subjects. As she described what her ideal Sikh woman would be, she went back to that night's reaction to her comment about gays and lesbians:

> Should your religion allow you to say things like this? I think that
> Sikhism says to question everything and then base your conclusions
> on love and acceptance. My ideal would be to confront all of those
> really dangerous topics and taboos. Confront it and then move on
> to how we are going to help in the long run. I was talking with this
> really straight guy, a baptized Sikh, and I was telling him about my
> work with AIDS patients. I told him about my ideas about sexuality,
> that everyone is on a continuum with heterosexuality at one end

and homosexuality at the other. As I was talking, I could see his face crashing because he had never imagined his sexuality could be on a continuum before! [Everyone in the room is cracking up.] In the end, I wound up asking him if he was a heterosexual by choice. He just mumbled something and walked away.

My ideal Sikh woman would not be afraid to tackle the areas of sexual abuse, domestic violence, and other taboo topics like their own sexuality. I believe this all leads back to self-respect, being able to step away from the crowd and stand up for what is right. These are the kinds of values Sikhism has given me.

I was enthusiastic about the potential for bringing to a wider audience what these young women were saying. At the same time, Cynthia and I both started wondering how others in the Sikh community (especially, elder males) would respond. No one had ever come forward publicly with these kinds of statements. But these young women were firm on the point that they wanted to get their views and experiences out there, where they could be discussed and heard, and where at least they might encourage Sikh girls growing up now that they too can think independently about their lives and their faith.

Having introduced the initial participants in this conversation—ourselves and thirteen Sikh women—we now move to specific thematic concerns: gender equality in Sikh tradition, the symbolism of the turban, and the social context in which North American Sikh women find themselves today. In no way do we claim that the people with whom we spoke are somehow "respresentative" of the Sikhs as a whole. Rather, we use the words of these women as an entry point to further discussion of the issues facing young, religiously inclined, gender-aware women of this community. In our concluding chapter, we ruminate further on the conjoining of feminism and ethnography as they play out in research *with* (not *on*) Sikh women. Other Sikh women, and some Sikh men, join our conversation as we move along.

2

Gender Equality in Sikhism

Countless are the ways of meditation,
  and countless are the avenues of love,
Countless the ways of worship,
  and countless the paths of austerity and sacrifice.
Countless texts, and countless the Vedic reciters,
Countless the yogis turning away from the world,
Countless the devout reflecting on virtue and knowledge,
Countless the pious, and countless the patrons,
Countless the warriors, faces scarred by iron,
Countless the sages sunk in silent trance.
How can I express the Primal Power?
I cannot offer myself to you even once.
Only that which pleases You is good.
You are forever constant, Formless One.

—excerpted from the Japji, verse 17. Composed by Guru Nanak;
translated by Nikky Gurinder Kaur Singh (1995:52–53)[1]

Sikhism: Religious Beliefs and Practices

The word *Sikh* in Punjabi means "disciple" and is derived from a Punjabi verb meaning "to learn." The Sikh tradition began on the Indian subcontinent in the fifteenth century with the teachings of its founder, Guru Nanak

---

[1] This is the first prayer in the Sikh holy book and is recited by Sikhs in morning devotions.

(1469–1539). A Sikh is understood to be a person who believes in One God or Ultimate Being, who is a part of all creation but transcendent of it, and who also follows the teachings of the Ten Gurus (Guru Nanak and his nine recognized successors), which are a part of the Guru Granth Sahib, or the Sikh holy book. To a Sikh, the Guru Granth Sahib is the Eternal Guru, which is why it holds such a special place in the *gurudwara* or, literally, "gateway to the Guru."

Although some religious scholars have written about the influences of Hinduism and Islam on the Sikh tradition, most Sikhs assert strongly that it is an entirely independent faith. It is a belief system in which every life is closely tied to communion with the transcendent; indeed, it has been called *orthoprax* rather than *orthodox* for this reason (Madan 1991). The principle of equality lies at the heart of Sikhism's ethical code; no distinction is to be made in terms of caste—central, of course, to the surrounding society in India—nor in terms of gender. Charity is another cardinal principle, as expressed in the symbolism of the "kettle" to feed the hungry. And most famously, the righting of injustice, as symbolized by the sword, is considered entirely of a piece with prayer and meditation. In Sikhism the intertwining of worldly and spiritual truths is axiomatic.

Although Sikhism is by and large not as well known as other so-called "world" religions, the numbers of Sikhs total somewhere between sixteen and twenty million. (This puts them approximately on a par with Jews, in demographic terms.) Most of these live in Sikhism's homeland, Punjab, but others live in other regions of the Indian subcontinent. In the past century, Sikhs have migrated to many other countries, settling heavily in Canada, the United Kingdom, and the United States. Many of these came as immigrants seeking economic opportunity, but since the 1980s others have come as refugees fleeing the bloody conflict that has engulfed Indian Punjab. The diasporan Sikh community is now as critical to Sikh consciousness as those who remain in the Punjabi homeland.

The notion of a historical and distinctive Sikh identity, from the Guru period (1500–1708) to the present day, is a hotly debated topic between some academic scholars and many in the worldwide Sikh community. (See, for example, McLeod 1989; Oberoi 1994.) For our interlocutors in this study, making a conscious choice "to be Sikh" is usually equated with conforming to the religious codes of conduct and beliefs of Khalsa, or "baptized" Sikhs, which includes the wearing of religiously significant symbols known as the five K's: the keeping of unshorn hair or *kes*, held in a topknot on top of the head by a *kanga* or small curved comb that can then be covered with a turban, and the wearing of special breeches or *kachera*, a steel bangle or *kara*, and a sword or *kirpan*. These are sometimes called the "five signs" of the Sikh, and they were given to the Sikhs by the last Guru, Guru Gobind

Singh.[2] Historically and today, not all Sikhs are "baptized" (also called **Khalsa** and sometimes "orthodox" Sikhs). But for some of the women with whom we spoke, becoming initiated as a member of the Khalsa is a step critical to establishing identity. They have "taken *amrit*," which means that they have undergone the ritual of imbibing the sacred nectar bequeathed by Guru Gobind Singh. *Amritdhari* Sikhs have special responsibilities and obligations, and take lifelong vows to follow the Sikh tenets.

While some scholars view the Sikhs who have been baptized into the Khalsa in this way as "fundamentalists," from the viewpoint of Khalsa Sikhs themselves they are simply being "true Sikhs" (*gursikh*). Since it has been Khalsa Sikhs who have formed the backbone of the separatist insurgency that has taken place in Punjab in the past two decades, the term "fundamentalist" to describe those who have taken *amrit* has acquired a heavy political connotation as well. We find this term relatively uninformative; the beliefs and behaviors of the *amritdhari* women we know are far more complex than can be elucidated by use of an accusatory label. This complexity will become clear as we hear their own descriptions of the initiation experience.

There are no specific age restrictions for the taking of *amrit*; it is left up to individuals and the parents of children to decide when they are ready for the ceremony and the religious commitments that go along with it. At the ceremony, the initiates are asked if they have been forced into it and if they are making this conscious choice on their own. According to Amanpreet, if the "Five Beloved Ones" who administer the initiation believe that anyone has been forced into it and may not have made his or her own choice, they have the obligation to stop the ceremony and tell the individual and his or her family that it is not the right time for this to take place.[3] *Amrit* requires a deep spiritual commitment on the part of the initiate and is not supposed to be undertaken lightly. Amanpreet found that her decision to take *amrit* and to commit fully to Sikhism was similar to the process of deciding to get married:

> I think the initiation ceremony is really the first step to becoming a Sikh. Until you make public commitment, it is as if you are just flirting with the Guru. In a sense it is like a marriage: There are certain vows that you take that you are supposed to live up to, and if you

---

[2] Note that there are some Sikhs who believe that the turban is one of the five signs (rather than the hair itself). One woman talks about this in chapter 3.

[3] When Guru Gobind Singh created the Khalsa or siblinghood of Sikhs in 1699, he identified five individuals as founders of the Khalsa, initiating them with *amrit* and then having them initiate him. So the five who administer baptism today are called Five Beloved Ones.

decide to leave this path then you have broken your commitment and the relationship can be anulled. Before you take this step initially, you have to ask yourself, do I really want this or should I decide not to take this path at all?

Surpreet, who had taken *amrit* with her family at the age of twelve, expressed some regret over being unable to keep the commitments of *amrit* while growing up and is trying to get back "on the path" after her marriage and first child:

> I was twelve when I took amrit with my family. Then over time my commitment kind of decreased. I started going to high school and university and had other influences, but now I wish I could get back onto the path. It just takes a dedication and a commitment to the religion. In some ways I am ready, but in other ways there are just minor things keeping me back like cutting my hair and tweezing my eyebrows, that kind of stuff. I know I will eventually get over this, but it is not out of my system yet. I wish I could leave that behind and get on the path.

Rajvinder described herself as coming from a Punjabi Sikh family who had little interest in religion. She described how the decision to take *amrit* has been a process:

> I have made a conscious choice to be a Sikh. In my family, religion wasn't really there unless you made an effort to make it a part of your life. You went to *gurudwara* on special occasions and when something was going on in the family. Personally I think it was an easy choice for me to make when it happened, but the building up to that point was a more difficult process. Psychologically you set up barriers and roadblocks for yourself along the way. But when it actually came time for me to take *amrit*, when I felt it was right, everything just worked out and life was a lot easier from then on. I think that my life has been more sensible and comfortable since then. I feel like I am really alive now.

Another Sikh woman also uses the metaphor of marriage to explain what the commitment is like:

> I compare committing to a faith to getting married. In my case, my groom is God, and for a man, his wife would be God. Initially, like many other Canadians, my parents introduced me to Sikhism. I was taught the faith from a young age, so I grew up learning about Sikhism. Just like growing up with the boy next door. And even though our parents might want us to get married, why would we marry each other simply because we grew up together?

Just because I was raised in this faith, doesn't mean that I don't have a choice in whether or not I want to commit to this faith. If you grew up with the boy next door, when it came time to marry you would still ask yourself whether he was the right man for you. Do you think that's a decision you could make as a child, or a decision you would be better equipped to make as an adult?

As I grew older, and came into my own as a woman, I started to ask myself if this faith was right for me. Up till then, I had passively chosen this religion. I had grown up with a Sikh background; I had not chosen this path. It had been given to me as a possible religion by my parents. But now as a woman, I needed to decide if I wanted to commit to this faith. After exploring this question seriously for a few years, I decided my answer was yes.

This description of making a "conscious choice" to be a Sikh was something that resonated with all the women in this group. They acknowledged that this part of their personal identity was socially constructed and did not believe that it was something they were born into. This contrasted with the responses from the older women in the community, who felt that because they had been born into Sikh families, it automatically made them "a Sikh." There was little or no talk of their religion being something that they had to make a choice about. Yet, women in Rajvinder's age group spoke extensively about the evolution of their faith and religious practice.

The difference here is that the second generation of women are growing up in the context of the wider North American society, where contemporary discourse is shaped by concepts like "choice" and "gender." This is a whole frame of thinking that is entirely alien to many of the India-born Sikhs. Although many of these women's families could be described as socially liberal in their treatment and expectations of their daughters, a tug-of-war still takes place between traditional South Asian gender norms and Western secular culture. Like countless other teenagers of all cultures, Rajvinder went through a period of rebellion during her adolescence. She specifically tied this rebellion to her present religious commitment, believing it gave her a sense of independence necessary to learn about Sikhism for her own reasons:

When I was little, I went to Sunday school [Khalsa school] every week. It was one of those things that our parents made us do, but I didn't enjoy it because I had no idea why I was doing it. We did hymn singing and stuff like that; it was a matter of routine but it really made no sense to me. The older I got, the more I felt that something was missing, there was something about all of this that I didn't understand and no one was able to tell me.

My grandparents were religious, but to a certain extent they were limited in their abilities to answer certain questions. I have had to search for myself for things to make more sense to me—that was after a very wild adolescence, though. I was a real rebel [laughing]! I think it was when I was fourteen or fifteen that I got crazy, something just happened in my head [laughs]! I did things that I wasn't supposed to; I knew the difference between right and wrong, yet to me doing wrong was sometimes not that big a deal. I know that my parents worried for some years, "What is going to happen to her?"

I was pretty wild until I was eighteen or nineteen, but even after that I still had a wild streak. Then I think that something inside of me started to change. I started to become more conscious of what I was doing and started to question things more. Things had stopped making sense, and then I kept searching and things started to make sense again. That wild streak has had some positive effects, though, as I am the first person in my really big family of one hundred sixty people, besides my grandfather, to take *amrit*. I think the fact that I had that wild streak, that sense of self-confidence, has helped me in taking a step like that in my kind of family.

I started to hang around a different group of people who I thought really had it together. This is when I first understood the importance of *sangat* [congregation]. That association with other Sikhs is very important, and it has definitely helped me because the more I enjoyed their company the more I began to search for my own faith.

I had always been a public speaker and been active in the community in various things, so I was hired to do this religious television program for young Sikhs. I really didn't know anything about **Sikhi** [the Sikh way]; I was just reading from a prepared script. I would run into people who would tell me what a great job I was doing, that the kids really loved it and were getting into Sikhism, and I was thinking the whole time they were talking, "Well, I am glad they are getting it, because I'm not" [laughs].

Then I moved away from home and lived by myself for a long time, and I think that helped me really be able to concentrate on what was important to me. I needed to reorganize my life to make it the way that I wanted to live. At that time I was in an area where I had no other Sikh friends and nobody I could talk to about Sikhi. This time was good for me because it reassured me that although I was away from the *sangat* and my friends, my faith had survived and grown without having that supportive environment.

Rajvinder's experience of rejecting Sikhism and family expectations during adolescence, only to embrace her cultural and religious heritage later, was common among the women interviewed in this study. For some it happened earlier than others, but few women felt that it had been their families' religious influences that had led them to Sikhism. This theme of temporary isolation and independence of decision was raised by women again and again, especially related to the decision to take *amrit*. Rajvinder described her experience taking *amrit* the most thoroughly:

> I can tell you what it is all about and what things mean and how things are done, but I can't really describe everything that happened or give you a really detailed idea of everything. I don't even think it is possible; it is just beyond words.
>
> First you come in and you're seated and everything is introduced to you. The Five Beloved Ones will start up the dialogue telling you about the Sikh code of conduct and everything else. During the course of the ceremony a sugar cube is put into the cast-iron pot. With the double-edged sword, the Five Beloved Ones will recite the scriptures as they kneel down, and, then, with one hand on the pot, everybody concentrates on the sacred nectar and five special verses are recited as the sword is constantly moved back and forth in the water.
>
> It is really interesting because I am one of these people who is awful at concentration and I am thinking, how am I going to stand there for that amount of time? But it was almost like you were not even in yourself; it is that out-of-body feeling. So from the minute I stepped into the room to the minute I stepped out, I felt really different. I had always thought that it was going to be an awesome experience, but it was really beyond that and really fascinating. There was a really strong presence of **Waheguru** [God]. I have never felt so connected to Waheguru until then and since then.
>
> Then after the verses are done and the nectar is prepared, each person goes up one by one and is splashed five times in their hair, in their eyes, and then you drink *amrit* five times cupped in your hands and you say, "Waheguru ji ka Khalsa, Waheguru ji ki Fateh" every time.[4] Then at the end all of the people who have taken *amrit* drink the remaining nectar and then walk around the Guru Granth Sahib. (I hope I am getting this all in order!)
>
> Afterwards the Five Beloved Ones stand there and when they talk to you it feels as though they are talking to an entirely different person because you have changed because of what you have just been through.

The *amrit* ceremony is sometimes likened to a Christian baptism because it was established to help move a disciple from the position of a community outsider to the status of religious community membership, and because it relies heavily on the notions of Divine grace and what religious

---

4 This phrase means "God's Khalsa, God's Victory" and is used as a greeting and motto of Khalsa Sikhs.

scholars call *ekstasis,* or feelings of spiritual ecstasy. (For a comparison of Sikhism and Christianity, see Cole and Singh 1993.) After the *amrit* ceremony, the community of believers who have already passed through this initiation recognize publicly this initiate's new status and community identity. As Rajvinder states at the end of the preceding passage, there is a heavy emphasis on identity transformation. The taking of *amrit* is a "rite de passage," in classic anthropological terminology.

For the women who were *amritdhari,* or baptized Sikhs, the initiation represented the beginning, not the end, of their spiritual journey. It was recognized that although one may go through the ceremony, it does not always bring about the expected feelings immediately. Daljot had felt she had been pressured into taking *amrit* for the first time by her father's well-meaning expectations. She realized afterwards that she had not been ready to receive "the Guru's grace" because she had not felt that sense of transformation of belief. Daljot linked her personal transformation to the second ceremony in which she took *amrit:*

> I made that choice to become a Sikh when I became baptized about four years ago. I believe that is when you truly define yourself as Sikh. Initially, I didn't really understand what was happening; my parents were pretty religious but I wasn't really into it. We went to *gurudwara* but that was about it, I didn't know anything about the philosophy or the basic principles and all of that.
>
> My dad started encouraging me to take *amrit,* but I figured I would do it one of these days but he really started putting the pressure on. I took *amrit* initially just to please him. I didn't know what I was getting into, but I figured "What the heck, it can't be too bad." I thought that now that I have taken *amrit,* my dad will be happy but I still wasn't curious about what I had done. I had just done it out of a sense of obligation. Some people I talked to said, "Oh, it is an amazing experience!" and I did not feel that when I first took it. It was just like we went through the motions but I didn't feel it in my heart. During the ceremony you are supposed to say and feel like you're giving your head to the Guru, but that was not how I felt. I was realizing that there must be something when people are saying this, right? I must have done something wrong.[5]
>
> That summer, we went to religious camp and that kind of changed my whole outlook. That is where I learned the spiritual side of the religion and figured out what the main purpose in life is

---

[5] "Giving your head to the Guru" refers to Guru Nanak's injunction that Sikhs who "want to play this game of love" should come to his street with their heads in their palms, that is, without ego. According to Sikh tradition, the original Five Beloved Ones who established the Khalsa gave their heads for Guru Gobind Singh.

and what we are here to do. I think this was a turning point in my
life, where I took another look inside of me and found out I had
taken *amrit* for the wrong reasons. The man at the camp said I
should take *amrit* again because I had made this new commitment,
so I didn't go through the whole ceremony again, I just drank the
amrit. I felt like finally I had taken the right step and that now I had
taken *amrit* for the right reasons. I really felt like this time I was
doing it from my heart. It was sort of a rejuvenation thing, sort of
like a second birth almost. I felt like I had really given myself and
my head to the Guru. When I came home from camp, I felt like
my life had changed. I started thinking about what I had to do to
achieve the goal of becoming a *gursikh* [true Sikh] and about why
I had been given this human life.

For me the taking of *amrit* was a first step. I have heard this anal-
ogy so many times and it always makes sense to me: In order to
enter something like a school, you have to wear a uniform, you have
to follow the rules and discipline, and then if you don't, you get
kicked out or something, right? So to me this uniform, this discipline, is just the entrance requirements and now I have to work
toward the Ultimate.

This working "toward the Ultimate" refers to an *amritdhari* Sikh's commitment to achieve union with the Divine. As Nikky Gurinder Kaur Singh
explains, "All beings emerge from the singular Truth, so the Ultimate is
within us all. But it is not sufficient simply to conceive the Truth; the truth
must be lived" (1995:9). The key component of this goal can be achieved
only by concentrating on the Name of the Ultimate. Devout Sikhs rise early
in the morning to recite prayers and to meditate on the Name; then in the
afternoon there are more prayers and again before retiring to bed. Daljot
explained some of the spiritual requirements or "rules" for *amritdhari* Sikhs
and confessed that she sometimes has a hard time living up to the ideals that
are set by the "strictest people":

When you are *amritdhari*, it is important to meditate on the Name,
which is the remembrance of God in your mind. When you begin
after taking *amrit*, you are supposed to do it regularly and devote
a tenth of the day to it, so that is typically two hours of meditation
and remembrance of God. How successful you are is not up to you;
it truly depends on the grace of God, you can just make the effort of
doing your part. If He wants you to excel spiritually, then it happens
to you. The word for God, "Waheguru," is given to you by the Five
Beloveds and you only get that through the *amrit* ceremony. So after
you have taken *amrit*, you are supposed to go into the repetition of
that Name and, although it is a long process as you keep doing it, it

leads to some fruition in your life. So that is the first step and I am still struggling with that [laughs].

The optimum time to do that repetition is in the morning and I can't get up! The strictest people say you are supposed to get up at two o'clock in the morning and because I am a college student I don't go to sleep until twelve! You know that whole crowd of guys at the retreat? They were like "You have to get up at two o'clock, otherwise you are not really doing it." So at the retreat we got up at two. I typically get up around seven thirty now, get up and do meditation for fifteen to twenty minutes, and then after I do my five daily prayers in the morning and that takes about an hour. I think I see two o'clock as my aim one day to get up every day but I am not there yet [laughs]."

Amanpreet felt that her perspective on this commitment to being *amritdhari* had changed over the years. As a teenager, her motivations for taking *amrit* and her decision to "become a Sikh" had been grounded in two important feelings: the conviction of gender equality that she felt was embodied by the religion and the peace she found in the quiet spiritual moments of early mornings in the *gurudwara*. Now she is aware that every time she bows before the Guru Granth Sahib, she is confirming her commitment to her faith and submitting her own will to the guidance of "the Ultimate One."

In a sense you recommit yourself every time you go to the *gurudwara*. When I bow before the Guru, it is an act of submission. I didn't have that perspective when I first committed myself twelve years ago; back then it was more of a feminist perspective and an intellectual perspective. Yet I remember getting a lot of peace from listening to Sikh hymns in those days, and I listened to them more than I do now. I was in *gurudwara* every day of my own choice and that is pretty unusual for teenagers. I would go early before my classes at six in the morning. I think that time is what really created the basis and roots for what I have today. It is in those teenage years that you wind up making a choice of which way you are going to go and you face the consequences later in your life.

When the women discussed which aspects of Sikhism had come to mean the most to them or which were the qualities of their faith they valued the most, the comments were diverse and ran the gamut from being a practical way of life, to being a source of spiritual comfort, to bringing a feeling of group strength and identity. Yet often the most common response related to the gender equality that women expected from their religion and the value of self-respect embodied in the faith:

HARINDER: That notion of self-respect was the first thing that Guru Nanak said before he ever introduced anything about Sikhism. He said you have to have self-respect. I think that it is a very open and important teaching for anybody, whether you are Sikh or not, that you have to have self-respect before anything else in this world. That and the equality of the religion is what is important to me.

SANDEEP: I feel that Sikhism is very much about self-love. If you love yourself, you are not going to be codependent in a relationship. I felt that I was taught as an Indian woman to be codependent; my mom did the best she knew how and she thought it was beautiful what she was teaching me. She believed and taught me that a marriage is only what the woman makes it and no marriage is going to last if the woman doesn't do what is necessary. She needs to be patient and let it work through and then it will pay out. I thought to myself, is it better to suffer through a bad marriage or abuse, how do you let that "work through"? To me the essentials of Sikhism have taught me to know how to stand for justice and to stand for justice for yourself. I am talking about that true love for yourself that is based on spirituality and the sense of equality that Sikhism is all about.

DALJOT: I think that what makes me unique as a Sikh woman is the equality—in the religion not the culture. It is a very free religion and it's not strict in terms of women not being able to do this or that and having to stay in the household. This is what has attracted me to the religion.

SURPREET: I feel very fortunate to be a Sikh woman. The equality that a woman has in this religion in comparison to other religions: What we have, other religions don't have. That always sticks in my mind, and it gives me encouragement when I am about to do something. In university I have Muslim friends who don't have that; they say that when they go to their mosques there are a lot of differences in what they are allowed to do and what the men are allowed to do.

We believe that these women are expressing an important trend in Sikh women of their age group and probably also class group. This singling out of gender equality and self-respect as primary reasons for younger women's attraction to Sikhism will be explored more deeply in subsequent chapters, but it is worth noting that this is not a focus that either men, or older women, typically emphasize. We believe that this association of Sikhism and gender equality among younger Sikh women is a key to understanding how these women have constructed their identities to highlight Sikhism above other possible identifications of Punjabi, Indian, South Asian, American, Canadian, and so on. It is also the driving force behind their personal goals and beliefs and is used as the justification for the challenging of culturally traditional gender expectations within the Punjabi Sikh community.

Figure 2.1   Sikhs worshiping in a *gurudwara*.

Women's Involvement in Religious Institutions

The most important institution in the Sikh community is the local *gurudwara*. Depending on the size of the community, there may be several in one major urban area and each possesses a distinct character. For example, in a given urban center, one may be known as "Khalistani," one "Old Family," one "Liberal," and so on. Sometimes they are linked to traditional caste affiliation (though anathema to Sikhism). *Gurudwaras* serve as arenas of religious worship, social gathering, and cultural/religious education (Figure 2.1).

Sikhism has no priests in the classic sense of the term. The *granthis*, or scripture-readers, conduct the worship services, and there are caretakers and management committees that administer the building and the congregation, but the social structure of the *gurudwara* is deliberately egalitarian in nature. Anyone may get up and speak or read from the Guru Granth Sahib, sing hymns and play religious music, or speak on any topic. Most Sikhs are quick to point out that women are free to participate in every aspect of religious life, but female *granthis* are rare. This is most likely due to the fact that, although held in esteem for their religious commitment, *granthis* are not typically paid well and their housing, like that of clergy of other religions, is often spartan when compared to that of many of their parishioners. The working hours of the *granthis* are long and often unpredictable, and for women this field is not very appealing when the added stresses of caring for children and family are thrown into the mix. A young, progressive *granthi* had been speaking out about making the religious training process more conducive to women so that they might be inclined to devote their lives to religious service. He commented, however, that typically it was not the kind of life that most Sikhs would wish for their daughters and there was little family encouragement for women to pursue this path. There are stories of qualified women candidates applying for the position of *granthi* in *gurudwaras* who have not been hired (for example, in California; see Kaur 1996). These stories make the rounds of the Sikh community and further discourage any women with similar ambitions.

Sikh institutional leadership has traditionally been patriarchal in nature, despite the religion's commitment to equity. But today many have started to recognize the necessity and benefits of including women in visible positions of power. Women are becoming a more common sight on *gurudwara* boards and community-service committees. Men in these *gurudwaras* speak with considerable pride that their institution has a woman or two on their executive committee, and they are quick to note that some *gurudwaras* even have women presidents. (See, for example, an entire book celebrating the accomplishments of Sikh women written by a male Sikh for the Sikh Missionary Society—Sidhu 1977.) During the period of this research, a woman was chosen to head the most important organization of Sikhs in India, the Shiromani Gurudwara Prabandhak Committee, or SGPC. But the discrepancy between these accomplishments and a record of full and equal participation by women is undeniable.

The women of this religious community, as is the case in many others, know that women's representation on boards and committees is in fact meager and that this representation often takes the form of "token" appointments with little real power. The younger women in North American congregations do take an active role in serving on various community-action boards, but they are often aware that they have been asked to join more as "a token Sikh woman" than a valued member whose opinions and talents are utilized. One woman acknowledged that she was being used on a committee on which she served as a visible signal to the younger Sikh community and the non-Sikh public that Sikh women hold an equal place in the religion and the community, but said that she knew her opinion and concerns were rarely sought or listened to by the older male members of the group. She felt she represented the second generation of recent Sikh immigrants who had educated their daughters to be spokespeople or "ambassadors" for the community in the larger North American context. This ambassador role and high visibility can and does lead to an increase in demands for actual—as well as symbolic—power sharing. Amrita Basu, who has studied South Asian women extensively, noticed this transition among Hindu nationalist women as well (Basu 1995:170–71). Since in the case of Sikhism it is clear that such power sharing is mandated by the faith itself, further progress in this area is highly likely.

The answer to the question "What roles do women fill in your *gurudwara?*" today, however, is most often that they serve in the community kitchen (*langar*) or that they play music and sing hymns.

SURJEET: Generally, women are allowed to do just about everything in the *gurudwara*. On a regular basis, though, they are allowed to do the singing or the reading from the Guru Granth Sahib, but you more often see men doing those jobs. Women help out in the upkeep and maybe serve on a committee.

HARMANJOT: In the *gurudwaras,* women are mostly in the kitchen. I see that many women are not baptized, so they are not allowed to prepare or serve *prashad* [the consecrated food distributed at places of worship]. I don't think it is proper that if a woman is not baptized that she is not allowed to serve. They should be able to do any service; if they want to serve in the kitchen, if they want to serve *prashad*, if they want to dust or clean something, that should be fine. But I think they are limited to the kitchen most often.

As anyone who has been to a *gurudwara* knows, men also serve in the kitchen preparing and serving meals. It is a way of establishing equality not only in gender roles but also in class and caste distinctions—distinctions that Sikhism also abhors. Pollution laws are a fact of life in Indian culture, and Sikhs have differentiated themselves from other religions of the region by insisting that in the Sikh *langar* everyone—men, women, children, high caste, low caste, rich or poor, even Sikh or non-Sikh—eats side by side and takes food prepared and served by anyone without pollution restrictions. This may not seem like a revolutionary idea to non-Sikhs, but in the cultural context of India, and South Asia in general, this is a tremendous statement of equality. This is seen as so important to the foundations of Sikh principles that violent *gurudwara* fights have resulted from an easing of the symbols of social equity within this eating ritual. Some *gurudwaras* in North America have tried to get their congregates to use chairs and tables in the community kitchens instead of everyone sitting on the floor as a sign of equal status of all, but have been met with strong resistance from some quarters because of the fear of an increase in caste/class/gender restrictions that might accompany such a move.[6]

---

[6] The table and chair issue is highly complex, related to power struggles between various groups of Sikhs. It became a highly divisive matter for North American Sikhs.

Religious Ideals Versus Lived Realities

Despite the general agreement that women are allowed to serve in any capacity and the lack of religious pollution laws associated with menstruation in Sikhism, we found that these younger women, who talk more freely about such topics, had experienced being told by men of their *gurudwaras* they may not serve in specific ways, related to the pollution attached to being female. When pushed, most Sikhs will agree that this rejection of any aspect of human anatomy and physiology, given by God, is totally anathema to the spirit of Sikhism. Yet:

HARMANJOT: I used to go to the *gurudwara* a lot and liked to do the fanning of the Guru Granth Sahib ji.[7] I was doing this one day and this guy came to me and said that I could not do this and I asked him why not. He said that since I cut my hair I was not allowed to. I said that I had cut my hair but that it said nowhere in the scriptures that I could not serve in this way. I told him to show me where it said this. He was really surprised that I fought with him about this; he expected that I wouldn't say anything and would just go away. But I really stood up to him and said, "Tell me who said that I couldn't do this!" He said it was the decision of the chairman of the *gurudwara* committee, so I told him that I would go and speak with the chairman.

Then he changed his tactics and said that it was really a problem because women were not clean and they could be sick—that is, menstruating—and shouldn't be serving because they were not clean. I told him that it was my business if I am clean or not and I was not going to share my hygiene with him because it was none of his business! I told him he was going to have to think up another reason why I couldn't serve. He said that I probably shaved my legs! I asked him how he would know if I shaved my legs or not and that, even if I did that, I still had the right to do the fanning if I wanted to!

I found after that, because I used to go alone, the men would make comments about how I was always alone and no one was accompanying me. I found that very discriminating, so now I try to go to *gurudwara* when I know that only a few people are there. I am not sure it really has to do with the *gurudwara* as a whole; I think it is just a group of men, mostly middle-aged, who decided that this guy was the one to approach me. It was an unfortunate decision for him [laughs]. He just thought I was going to say OK and go away. I would never do

---

[7] The holy book on its throne is ritually fanned, as a king would be in traditional India.

that, though; I would never sit there and let someone give me crap about something that is not true.

SUKHMINDER: I like to perform the religious music at the *gurudwara,* and I have been told by people that you can't do that on those days when you are not clean; you can't go and bow in front of Guru Granth Sahib when you are not clean. I thought this was really weird because if we are not clean, why would God give us these functions? It is just a ridiculous idea. I was at a workshop and I asked about this issue. Our mentors there said flat out that you could be on your menstruation and you could do whatever you want because that was a part of the equality of Sikhism. But I know that at Harmandir Sahib [the "Golden Temple"] in Amritsar, one of my friends went and she was *amritdhari.* They do the processional thing of bringing the Guru Granth Sahib in and out and usually the men carry it. She asked since it was her first time there if she could help to carry it and she was told no. When she asked why, since she was *amritdhari* and it shouldn't be a problem, she was told that it just doesn't look good for one woman being in that group with all of the men. She was very hurt because she had traveled so far to come there and it was one of her dreams to do that. She was told that she could not do this in our Golden Temple. I thought this was such hypocrisy on their part in terms of what we are taught and what they actually do.

DALJOT: I was at a retreat where one of the preachers said that the problem with women being discriminated against in *gurudwaras* was the result of women's attitudes as well as men's. He said that women just don't want to get up and take a stand on those issues or they don't know that they can get up and challenge men on these issues. They are scared of what people might think or what their husband will say. They are afraid of their family being ashamed and being shunned by the community or something.

I think that we as Sikhs need to change the way preaching is done in many of the *gurudwaras.* There are a lot of preachers who come here from India, and when they preach they still have that mentality in their preaching that women are inferior. Whenever a boy is born in the family, they come to the *gurudwara* and celebrate about how great it is that a son has been born. But, on the other hand, when a girl is born there is no such speech in the *gurudwara.* It starts with the *gurudwara* because it is the central institution in the religion. If they preached what the Gurus taught in their time, then this whole attitude has a chance of changing. I believe that this education has to come from the *gurudwaras.* I know that my mom's generation, many of them are not educated or not as educated and so a lot of them believe a lot of the stuff these preachers say. I think it would be a big revolutionary step to change things if the preachers actually preached what the Gurus taught.

I have never seen any professional women preachers, but there are women who will get up and speak in *gurudwara*. They are all from the younger generation. I think it is the younger generation of women who will make the difference because they understand the issues and they have the knowledge and courage to get up and take a stand. We have a problem, though, relating to the older generation of women.

The preceding observations by Daljot for the continuing preference for male children among Sikhs are echoed by many North American Sikh women. The preference for male children is a phenomenon found around the world and especially in the classically patrilineal, patrilocal societies of South Asia. Female infanticide has always been condemned in Sikh tradition, but the preference for males over females is still an ever-present reminder of the underlying negative feelings toward women in the wider culture. Many of the women we interviewed said that their own families were very progressive and that their parents valued them as much as their brothers. Yet they all knew of many cases where families were congratulated on the birth of a son and consoled at the birth of a daughter. This practice was not as much of a factor among younger people, but the older generation was said to have held on to the practice of celebrating a male birth with a continuous reading of the Guru Granth Sahib in the local *gurudwara* or in the home and by passing out sweets to the community and friends. In the case of a female, families celebrated only privately. For some, this disjunction carries through to later birthday parties as well.

In one family, the Dodge Caravan they drove was decorated with a "My Son Is an Honor Student" rear window sticker, though the daughter was also an honor student. A sign of the times and the place: The *son* eventually persuaded the parents to add in print MY DAUGHTER IS AN HONOR STUDENT.

Gender Backlash and Its Effects

Deeply embedded patriarchy, whether cultural or religious in origin, can lead to a backlash as women speak out on issues ranging from domestic violence to women sharing power in *gurudwaras*. As was related in some of the narratives, Sikh women are often told they are not allowed to participate in certain aspects of religious life, although there may be no scriptural precedent for this exclusion. Women are told they may not hold positions of power and are given misogynist interpretations of Sikh scripture and history by certain men in the community to back up their authority (see Basu

1995:174). Jasvinder, for example, related a story about how damaging this contradiction between religious ideals and cultural biases can be to a young woman's faith. She thought that she was respected as an equal member in her religious community, but there have been incidents through which she realized just how illusory that community commitment to gender equality can be:

> There was a woman running for president of the *gurudwara* and this whole issue about women's roles in the *gurudwara* started up. Of course, I decided to make a speech [laughs]! But it ended up that one of my girlfriends got up and read the verse that says "Why condemn her that gives birth to kings?" and then continued into this whole discussion about how women should be treated as equals.[8] Well, the plan was she was going to read the verse in Punjabi and then I would translate for people into English and talk about it. We made our presentation and an uncle came up and asked why we had chosen to use that verse, since it said that woman "gives birth to kings" not queens! It was frustrating that it didn't work the way we wanted it to. Afterwards, students in my Khalsa school class stopped coming. I was really hurt when [the parents] started keeping their daughters out of my class and telling them that I wasn't a good role model. I was trying so hard to be a good Sikh sister and a good role model.

Many Sikhs have suggested in their comparisons between Sikh and other Punjabi groups' treatment of women (read Hindu or Muslim) that Sikhs can be viewed as "more civilized." This can be found in the assertions of Sikh literature that extol the virtues of the status of women in Sikhism. In some ways, some Sikhs employ the same model of gender comparison as British colonialists did against Indian nationalists when they cited, for example, practices like the ritual immolation of widows to denounce the entire culture as barbaric. Contemporary Hindu nationalists do the same today when they conceive themselves as morally superior to Muslims because of the perceived powerlessness of Muslim women. In other words, how magnanimously a society treats its most powerless members (women, children, elderly, slaves, disabled, etc.) is used as a measure of the virtue of the whole society. Often the "morally superior" accusers do not examine their own gender practices in the realities of the daily lives of ordinary women but, rather, use the other's gender transgressions as a way to portray their own

---

[8] This is a statement attributed to Guru Nanak: "It is through women that order is maintained. Then why call her inferior from whom all great ones are born?" It is commonly brought up whenever gender equality in Sikhism is under discussion.

community as more "woman friendly," hence more civilized. All Sikhs are proud of their enlightened ideas about gender equality—none more so than the men in power!

Women like Jasvinder often experience the backlash against holding their religious communities to their stated ideals of gender equality. They are isolated or gossiped about as a form of social censure for unacceptable behavior. Real women bear the brunt of the community's lip service to an ideal it does not meet (see Papanek 1994). Even producing a book that relates such behaviors, however much in the interests of affirming the ultimate ideals of Sikhism and the adherence of young Sikh women to them, will surely provoke controversy among traditionalists. We, and the women who participated in the making of this book, ask them to accept this offering in the spirit of dialogue toward growth rather than as criticism. Every religion has to struggle to live up to its ideals.

Religion and Feminism

The types of "frontal attacks" on beliefs about gender equality in the Sikh community, as related here, are only one of the ways that younger Sikh women are challenging the status quo. Another way of confronting patriarchal practices and beliefs within the community is by using religiously based definitions of feminist principles. These younger women are holding Sikh men up to their religious principles and working for long-term results:

RAJVINDER: Personally, I don't think that being a Sikh man or woman should be all that different, although it often is. Ideally, they should have the same goals and the same lifestyle. I think that Guru Gobind Singh was a staunch feminist! People always get scared when I use that word [laughs]. I think that my personal definition of feminism is anybody who is committed to and believes in the inherent equality between the genders. That does not mean that you have to abandon what you are comfortable with in order to be equal. If you are comfortable with your role as a housewife and taking care of the children and doing it of your own free will, then that is just as valuable as anything that other women have chosen to do.

In the preceding narrative passage, Rajvinder states her own definition of feminism as the belief in "the inherent equality between the genders" and links this belief with Guru Gobind Singh, the tenth and last Guru and the founder of the Khalsa or siblinghood of the pure, into which Sikhs are initiated through the taking of *amrit*. The concept of Guru Gobind Singh as a "staunch feminist" is not something one would hear from many in the Sikh community. Rajvinder acknowledges the negative associations her community has with the "F-word" and probably uses it at least partially for shock value. She uses it to shock Western secular notions of feminism by calling an eighteenth-century religious leader a precursor to modern feminist ideas, and for her own community the statement brands her as a rebel for linking one of the most important Sikh Gurus to such a reputedly antireligious, antifamily philosophy. She then goes on to qualify her definition of feminism as a matter of choice: Women should not feel compelled to give up traditional roles as caretakers or housewives but should be free to choose how to wield their equal power within the community.

There are a few examples of Sikh women embracing both their religion and feminist principles at the same time. Nikky Gurinder Kaur Singh is perhaps the most widely known scholar on Sikhism's scriptural and philosophical positions on gender equity. Her major work, *The Feminine Principle in the Sikh Vision of the Transcendent* (1993), is unique in its academic treatment of Sikh scriptures from a feminist perspective. She highlights the actual translations of the Punjabi scriptures to show the purposeful projection of a gender-neutral concept of the Divine from the first Guru to the last. Another major point she makes is that all Sikhs are described in the scriptures as being like women longing for their bridegroom, in relation to the Divine. Marie-Aimee Helie-Lucas has found that this is also a rising trend among Muslim feminists, philosophers, and theologians; instead of buying into monolithic definitions of women's "historic" roles in Islam, they return to the original Arabic sources of scriptures for feminist interpretations of Islamic history and its context and to recover a sense of power and voice from within the religious framework (1994:401).

The young women whose words form the centerpiece of this study can be seen as Sikhs who have acquired the double advantage of holding both the "symbolic capital" of Sikhism (they commit to orthodox values and symbols) as well as the "cultural capital" of the larger North American society through their education and associations with non-Sikhs. This is a doubly empowered group of women, whatever hurdles they face in both arenas in which they operate. There is certainly no attempt by these women to isolate themselves or to retreat to a purely Sikh or Punjabi world. Their private lives may be lived there, but they are publicly integrated into the larger Anglo-dominated cultures of the United States and Canada. They know how to negotiate and link these two worlds with much more success than the senior members of their congregations. Indeed, we believe that these young women are well placed to lead the complex and dynamic Sikh community into the future as a key component of our North American cultural mosaic.

3

Living Up to the Turban

I took the saliva-darkened cord, pulled it back where my hair bun
   rested low and tucked it up
over the turban, just as you do.
In the mirror I saw my father as he must have looked as a young boy,
my teenage brother as I remembered him,
you as you face Canada,
myself as I need to be.
The face beneath the jaunty turban began to smile.
I raised my hands to my turban's roundness, eased it from my head
   and brought it before me,
setting it down lightly before the mirror.
It asked nothing but that I be worthy of it.

—*Shauna Singh Baldwin, "Montreal 1962" in*
English Lessons and Other Stories *(1996:16)*

Identity

The term "identity" is used broadly in most conversational arenas today and includes notions of race, class, gender, ethnicity, belief systems, world views, ideologies, and religions. In terms of this last factor, the latter part of the twentieth century has seen an unexpected revitalization. Many prominent thinkers prior to World War II had expected religiously based identities to decline as the world "got smaller" and as science explained many of the mysteries previously embedded in the sphere of the sacred. While secularization certainly happened at the metropolitan centers of the world, at the peripheries religion became mobilized as critical to resistive identities.

    The recent revival of the strictest form of Sikhism has been linked to the politics of Sikh separatism, with men wearing turbans symbolizing political radicalism in some circles. What our study shows is that women may have different reasons than men for a renewed interest in the turban. For many Sikh women, it is a symbol related as much to gender as to politics or faith. The concept of "Sikh identity" is not monolithic. Women's side of the identity question has barely been explored.

The concept of a *gursikh* (true Sikh) in Sikhism is a man or a woman who is *amritdhari,* a member of the Khalsa community, and who follows all the principles of the Gurus. In the excerpted narratives of the Sikh feminine ideals as defined by the women themselves, we find that central in the descriptions of the female *gursikh* is the **dastaar,** or turban, which is one of the most visible symbols associated with the Khalsa. Although it is classically associated with men, the women who are putting on turbans now are expanding its connotation to include women as well. This wearing of the turban and its association with demands for gender equality can be seen as an example of the fluidity and flexibility in constructions of gendered identities and how symbols in the cultural repertoire are used and manipulated by these women as forms of agency. The renewed use of the turban among women is not mere adherence to tradition, or a backward-looking "fundamentalism." These women are using a traditional symbol to reflect changing ideas about gendered identities in Sikhism, which has opened up a dialogue about representation, power sharing, and the dynamics of the *siblinghood* (classically, "brotherhood") of Sikhism.

The Ideal Sikh Woman

When women interlocutors were asked to describe the characteristics of a Sikh woman as opposed to just a Sikh, these were some of the responses:

JASJIT: The ideal Sikh woman would be an *amritdhari* Sikh woman who is raising her kids not only to be Sikhs but also to take an active role in society as well as the community. She would try to make herself the best possible person she could be.

DALJOT: In today's society the ideal woman for me would be . . . she doesn't have to have a career. I think that Western society puts too much emphasis on that. She would be a strong woman, one who is independent and who can choose to have a career, or if she is staying home, she can be just as much my role model, if she is taking care of her kids and everything. If she is internally happy and she is trying to achieve the aim of her life, then she is the ideal that I would follow.

HARINDER: I would say she would have to have, first and foremost, that which was given to us by Guru Nanak ji, self-respect. Anybody, especially a woman, who doesn't have self-respect, doesn't have respect for anything else . . . that is the main thing, she has to have respect for herself, she has to be honest to herself before she can be honest with anyone else. I feel that in itself is hard to maintain, for myself. I think that other than that she just has to be true to herself and follow the words of the Gurus according to herself, not to what she has been told by other people. You know you grow up in *gurudwaras* and people preach to you and it took me a long time to understand that these people who are teaching you stuff could be wrong . . . and they are not always right. In Sikhism there is no intermediary, it is you and the Guru; you are free to make your own distinctions of what you feel is right and wrong.

SANDEEP: I had read this Internet posting once that meant a lot to me and it had so many descriptions of what the ideal Sikh woman would be, and to be able to read that and compare it with my own life was really interesting. In regard to the religious angle of it . . . from the aspect of what the Gurus were trying to tell us as opposed to what the culture tells us . . . I mean I realize that obviously no one is going to be living in the ideal or that it would be very difficult . . . and that it is just my point of view. I would not want to see what we would think of as the politically correct ideal of the Sikh woman, and I think there is definitely an "ideal" gap across generations.

There is nothing wrong with a politically correct version but it just . . . it is someone that is very active, doing the political stuff, getting involved in the political aspects. She is very knowledgeable about the spiritual aspect and is taking that aspect a step further, maybe wearing a turban or something.

Everyone is going to have their own ideas about the characteristics or qualities or what they see a Sikh woman should conform to. This posting is so interesting because it was done as a list of qualities of a Sikh in general not really referring to a woman in particular, but the person who wrote it used "she" so that's why it has made such an impact on me.

[She reads from a copy of an anonymous e-mail post.] "She is a liberal individual; rigidity and stubbornness do not make up her character. She remains proactive and accepts the entire creation and millions of varieties and forms which all contain the same essence (the Divine spirit). She remains a servant and completely aware without placing judgment because everything that occurs is part of the Lord's plans. She uses introspection and truth as her guides, she remains steadfast on the path of the Guru, and keeps her heart attached to the Masters' feet in complete submission to the will. Strength and perseverance compose her internal architecture with rooms full of compassion, sensitivity, and love. She places no expectations on the outside world, remaining devoid of anger, resentment, frustration, fear, disappointment, and worry. She has devoted her life to service for the Lord and has received great grace through her Guru."

Obviously, that is just talking about the spiritual side of things. I think those qualities and honesty and commitment, that internal strength, just having the self-confidence and self-respect, are so important. Not putting yourself down if something goes wrong or looking for the fault within you. I mean you have to do some introspection to make yourself a better person, but it is having that self-respect and treating yourself well where you have enough self-confidence to feel that your opinion matters and that you have the right to feel and have the right to express your feelings and you have the right to be a person and a part of the community.

TARANJEET: I don't feel like I fit the Sikh woman ideal and I think it is because I feel like "Oh, it's the women who have the turbans," and I felt that was the ideal Sikh woman. Even when we were at the women's retreat, there were a lot of women with the turban, not just the turban, but much more religious and much more knowledgeable; they took the time to know about politics and the human rights issues and all of these things and I thought this is the ideal Sikh woman.

I really felt inadequate. I think that someone brought up this point, that if you think differently about the politics or human rights, then you are in the minority and there was this unsaid pressure to conform. I know that the people who were at this retreat did not intend it to be this way, but I felt like I was on the other side of all of this and there was so much pressure on what the ideal is.

My totally personal idea of qualities for a Sikh woman would be courage, having that strength to stand up to anything. Love everyone, love that is unconditional and all-encompassing. I guess also that commitment to the Guru, the greater whole. Being a Sikh woman, you can focus that commitment to your husband, brothers, parents, and family and try to make that connection close and true. I sometimes falter in that connection; I put conditions on that connection. I sometimes feel it is broken, but it is never really broken. I would just need to commit myself to maintaining that connection, wholeheartedly above all else. I guess that connection is my ideal.

The *Dastaar* and Its Mixed Messages

As this research progressed, it became clear that the *dastaar*, or turban, was a vital piece of many Sikh women's identities and conceptions of ideal womanhood. There were multiple messages being actively sent by this practice to very different audiences, and this is evident in many of the descriptions of the "ideal Sikh woman," where the turban is mentioned as a symbol of group membership and religious commitment. There are also stereotypes within the Sikh community surrounding women wearing this traditionally male symbol that relate to gendered identity roles and how women actively use religious and cultural symbols to secure greater gender equality within their own communities as well as greater ethnic recognition in the dominant "white" society.

Most of the women we spoke with felt that the decision to wear the *dastaar* was a process of reevaluating their identity as *amritdhari* Sikhs. Only Harmanjot, Amanpreet, Rajvinder, and Daljot were currently wearing turbans, however. Jasjit described herself as in the process of starting to wear one as she had taken to wearing a headscarf all the time to get used to the idea. But the subject of the turban came up because we were focusing on Sikh identity in general and the importance of initiation into the Khalsa. For these women the turban, the Khalsa identity, and Sikhism were inextricably linked with their personal identity. When Jasjit responded to the question "What is Sikh identity?" she said:

> It is more than just being religious; even if you are *amritdhari* on the inside, you can't always tell from the outside. I think that we women have to fight hard to know our Sikhi. Unless I wear the turban, I will never be recognized as a Sikh.

This is a reflection of the fact that Sikh women are not immediately recognizable as Sikh and may be mistaken for an unidentifiable South Asian woman in North America. Jasjit spoke of the frustration of being mistakenly identified as a Muslim or Hindu woman, whom she knows are associated in "white culture" with stereotypical passivity. The men of this community who are *amritdhari* are immediately recognizable as Sikhs because of the turban and beard; women who are *amritdhari* may keep all the symbols of the Khalsa but not receive the same level of identity recognition and perhaps community prestige as their male counterparts.

The formation of the male Sikh identity starts at an early age with the keeping of the uncut hair in a small covered topknot. In North America, this sets Sikh boys apart and there is much youth work done to help boys adjust to their very different look. For example, there are turban-tying contests and children's books celebrating boys with topknots. For girls, however, there is little training involving identity, other than to reinforce the point of not cutting one's hair. Among Khalsa Sikhs, girls' hair is typically grown long and then is often braided simply in the style of many South Asian women. Rajvinder said it was her work with Sikh youth that led her to reexamine her identity as a Sikh:

> I was always telling the little boys to be proud of who you are. I remember telling them, "Guru Gobind Singh ji made you stand out to be outstanding. That is one of the things you always have and you carry it with you. If you have hard times because people really think you are different, and it's hard to be different, you have to remember that is what makes you who you are and you have to be proud of that." And the more I said that, the more I realized that I didn't really grow up feeling that way.

Daljot spoke of the importance of her private commitment to Sikh teachings being reflected publicly through the wearing of the turban. When asked about Sikh identity, she replied:

> If the men of the community are going to wear a turban, then why shouldn't the women? In that sense, the outer appearance and the wearing of a *dastaar* is very important to me. On the other hand, if we're just doing it for the outer identity, then that's not acceptable. You have to be living up to that outer appearance because that outer appearance signifies something about you. It says you are a religious person, you've taken *amrit* and you're following the ideals. You have to live up to those standards you are portraying to the world outside.

The preceding quotes illuminate how much these women associate their wearing of the *dastaar* with their following Guru Gobind Singh's intentions of setting *amritdhari* Sikhs, both men and women, apart through the use of public symbols to communicate private religious emotions. The turban binds together in unity the *amritdhari* Sikh to her Guru and to her Khalsa through this public/private identity symbol.

Turban tying varies throughout South Asia and the Middle East, but some styles reflect the identity of a distinctive group. Sikh men have several characteristic turban styles that set them apart from Muslims or Hindus wearing turbans. Among South Asian women in general, it is unusual to wear a turban as it is almost exclusively a male symbol. In fact, the Sikhs as a whole are perceived by other communities as "masculine," the image of a turbaned and bearded male Sikh being almost the definition of masculinity on the subcontinent. Women who do cover their heads more commonly use a headscarf—associated with a certain reserve and humility.

The Sikh women who do wear a *dastaar* tie it noticeably differently than Sikh men. It is a much more understated look—tied close to the face—

than some of the common male turban styles. There are a few colors that symbolize certain attitudes, such as saffron being associated with a willingness to martyr (and today, sympathy with the Khalistan movement) and deep blue with the Akali Dal political party, but we have not seen any women consciously wearing *dastaars* of these colors to convey those messages. The women we know seem to be wearing any color turban according to their own taste and sense of style. Many wear basic black.

For some of the women, it was a difficult decision to start wearing a *dastaar* and be recognized as different from a more traditionally gendered appearance. Often women like Rajvinder say they are supported by a male religious teacher or friend who counsels them on their options:

> I thought it was hard. All of a sudden I'm going to be really different and people are going to have their eyes on me and I am going to be the different person in the crowd.
>
> Then my friend said, "Even when you get ready in the morning, you try to impress yourself and other people. You want to look prepared. Well, if in all that you are doing, you could include Guru Gobind Singh ji standing there, how would you want him to see you? If he said, 'This is my daughter,' how would you want to look? This is the person you are really trying to impress and make happy."
>
> That really had a big impact on me and I thought it made a lot of sense. I asked myself, "What am I really doing? What is my life really geared toward?"

When Rajvinder asks these questions, she is asking herself, "How well do I really understand what it means to be a Sikh of the Guru, if I am afraid to stand out as a Sikh?" This notion of a unique and separate public symbolic identity is essential to these women's understanding of their Sikh faith.

The turban is seen in the cultural context of the Sikh community as an outward sign of commitment but also as a sign of respect and power. An explanation of the unshorn hair and the binding of the turban offered by a popular primer is that it becomes, for Khalsa Sikhs, a uniform "which is both inexpensive and dignified" (Mansukhani 1977:31–32). The sense of dignity comes from the prevailing use of the turban as a sign of power and respect worn by Mughal kings and warriors at the time that Sikhism developed. A turban was also a hiding place for weapons and became a vital part of ritual language: "Oaths were sworn on turbans and . . . even today a man will indicate his submission to another by placing his turban at the other's feet," writes Christi Merrill of Rajasthan (1991:675). Among some groups of Islamic warriors, the turban is seen as a mobile shroud, implying the willingness of a soldier to martyr himself for God at any time. Guru Gobind Singh, with the action of creating the turban-wearing Khalsa, used the traditional meanings of public symbols and put them in a new context: The head and the hair retain the meaning of spiritual and temporal power (the yogi with matted hair, the Buddhist monk with shaved cranium) but not through renunciation. Instead, the power comes from a Khalsa Sikh using his head and hair as a public symbol of his allegiance to the orders of his Guru and his commitment to remain very firmly in the world while he is seeking spiritual salvation. The long hair (spirituality) bound into a turban (military readiness) was the new Sikh. This picture of a pious believer, ready at a moment's notice to defend the principles of his or her faith, is called by the Sikhs *sant-sipahi*, or saint-soldier. Since Guru Gobind Singh's time, this has been the ideal image of the Khalsa—an army of men and women committed to attaining spiritual and temporal liberation.

It is important to remember that men and women were not given separate codes of conduct by the Guru on that critical day in 1699 when the Khalsa was created, and this reflects the spirit of gender equality among the Sikhs going back to Guru Nanak. The only slight modification made for women was that they were not required to wear the *dastaar* to keep their hair neat and orderly. In most scriptural interpretations, women are told that as *amritdhari* Sikhs they must keep all the symbols of the Sikh faith but are not required to wear the *dastaar*. Although our interlocutors allude to Sikh women wearing the turban during the formation period of the Khalsa, it is difficult to find references to women being told how to keep their hair or wear their turban for this period. Yet, in the eyes of contemporary Sikh women, this absence suggests that all Sikhs, men or women, were included in the Guru's commandments and provides weight to their assertion of gender equality within Sikhism.

It should be noted that there is some controversy regarding the origins of the keeping of unshorn hair and the turban among Khalsa Sikhs and the scholars who study the evolution of Sikhism as a religion. A scholar who has done a great deal of work analyzing Sikh ideology, ritual, and social practices is W. H. McLeod. He asserts that the keeping of the hair and turban came through the dominant influence of Jat Sikhs (an agricultural caste) who practiced these habits prior to the founding of the Khalsa. He believes that the scriptural codes of conduct and dress attributed to Guru Gobind Singh, according to Sikh tradition, were historically not pronouncements that took place at the founding of the Khalsa. They were instead an evolution of identity that was prescribed by the dominant Jat Sikhs onto the other caste groups found in the early Sikh community (McLeod 1989). This is a problematic interpretation for Khalsa Sikhs as it denies the uniqueness and authority of texts attributed to Guru Gobind Singh. It also suggests that the Sikh identity contains less symbolic meaning and more political maneuvering by a dominant caste group, asserting its own identity as the only acceptable one for Sikhism.

Although members of the Sikh community are all in agreement that the Gurus intended that men and women were to be equal in social status, many of the women related in the previous section that this was truer in religious ideals than in daily practice. Some, like Rajvinder, felt that Sikh women might be at fault for giving up their equal identity, symbolized by the turban, in earlier times:

> We women were given a very equal position; we were given a very big responsibility, but we have stepped back. I thought, if I am going to have the responsibility of being a Sikh, then I want the privilege too. Wearing a turban is a privilege because of the identity that goes with it. You're recognized by the Sikh community and the outside and I wanted that for myself.

There are several religious teachers in the Sikh community today who advocate universal turban wearing as a means to differentiate the Sikhs clearly from the surrounding Hindu society in India, which some fear could eventually "swallow up" the Sikhs. This is not entirely an unreasonable fear, as it is essentially what has happened to Buddhism and to many of the indigenous tribal religions of the subcontinent. Today, there are Hindu nationalists who have this encapsulization as an explicit aim; recently, members of the ultra-nationalist Hindu RSS underwent the *amrit* ceremony. In the context of Sikhism as a minority population in the sea of humanity dominated by the overarching label of "Hindu," it may become politically necessary to differentiate one's identity and practices from the dominant majority. If, historically, it was the woman, "her role in the family and the normative gender constructions which formed the core of Brahminical ideological practices," as Sucheta Mazumdar contends, then it would make sense that Sikhs, in Punjab or in diaspora, would equally use women's identity in opposition to the "Brahminical Other" (Mazumdar 1994:250–253).[1]

In private reflections of women on their identity, a woman's *dastaar* appears to be associated with the constructing of an individual identity as well as a private understanding of her faith. The *dastaar* embodies the responsibilities of a Sikh to her religion and all the rights and responsibilities that go along with that recognition. But, like many symbols, the *dastaar* is multivalent: It has internal and external meanings and sends varying signals to varying audiences.

A Sikh woman known to Cynthia from her human rights work took a firm position on the turban question, giving a distinctly different view from the other women in this project:

---

[1] Cynthia has written extensively about the dynamics of Hindu expansion in India; see, for example, Mahmood 1993.

When I was a little girl and I asked why we Sikhs had to wear turbans, I was told that the turban is part of the Sikh uniform as required by Guru Gobind Singh. This got started during the time of our Ninth Guru, Guru Tegh Bahadur. It was the time when the Hindus were being forcibly converted to Islam, and a delegation of Kashmiri Pandits [Hindu Brahmins] came to our Guru and asked for his help. Guru Tegh Bahadur went to the Mughal ruler with two of his friends to plead their case. When he arrived, he too was asked if he would convert to Islam. He said no. The Mughal ruler then ordered that one of his friends have his fingers cut off joint by joint. Still, Guru Tegh Bahadur would not convert. His other friend was then sawed in half with a hacksaw. Guru Tegh Bahadur still refused to budge. He was then boiled in a cauldron, for how long I do not recall. After he was taken out of the cauldron (sic), he was asked again if he would convert. He said no and was beheaded. Many say, as his head was severed from his body, a piece of paper flitted to the ground. On it was written, "You may have my head, but you'll never have my faith." Guru Tegh Bahadur's head was brought to his son, Gobind Rai (who later became our Tenth Guru, Guru Gobind Singh), and the son inquired whether there hadn't been any Sikhs there that day to help his father. "I don't know," the bearer said. "You couldn't tell who was a Sikh and who wasn't." Gobind Rai then vowed that he would create a uniform such that out of thousands you would be able to spot a Sikh. Never again would a Sikh be able to hide from his or her responsibilities. The turban, along with the other four "signs," is part of that uniform.

Many Sikhs believe that the fifth sign is the *keski* [turban] not the *kes* [unshorn hair] and that it is required by both males and females.[2] Growing up, I never questioned this sign. Both my mother and my father wear turbans. So do all my *amritdhari* uncles and aunts on my dad's side of the family. My mother's side of the family was in India while I was growing up. I, along with other girl children of *amritdhari* families, grew up wearing a turban.

We all grew up understanding that the fifth *kakkar* ("K," referring to the five signs that all begin with the letter K) was the turban. It is the most visible *kakkar*. Without it, it is possible for the Sikh to hide in a crowd of thousands. If a woman is not wearing a turban, I often can't tell if she is *amritdhari* or not. The *kanga* and *kachera* are worn under your clothes. Usually, the *kirpan* is also worn under the clothes. The *kara* (wristband) on the other hand is worn by many people who are not baptized. So you can't tell from these other signs who is or is not a baptized Sikh.

---

[2] This is a minority view among Sikhs today and is identified with a group called the Akhand Kirtni Jatha, female members of which consistently wear turbans. The individual speaking here is not a member of this organization, however.

I compare taking *amrit* to getting married. Just as the wedding ring indicates that a person is married, the five signs indicate that I am married to God. As a married person, one has made vows in front of God and society. And society is aware that you have made those vows by looking at your wedding ring. By looking at that ring, they can tell when you have broken those vows. The five K's together are like a wedding ring. They show that a Sikh is married to God and that vows were made in front of God. And people can easily identify you as a Sikh because of the fifth K, the turban, and they can see whether you are somebody who is breaking the vows or not. Because of this uniform that Guru Gobind Singh has given us, it is hard for a Sikh to hide from his or her responsibilities. The degree of accountability becomes very high when one is so identifiable.

The most obvious public audience is the one that shares the common knowledge of the symbol's meaning—in this case, it would be the Punjabi Sikh communities to which these women belong. Typically, the reactions that the women got from this community once they started wearing the *dastaar* have been mixed:

When you start to break away from the status quo, you're being rebellious and that makes people uncomfortable. But many people have been very welcoming. I find that older men, especially the older men who spent most of their lives in Punjab, who are very traditional, have been terrific. Grandfathers have been the first to say this is excellent. A lot of women have been concerned, though. They want to know what are you going to do, how are you going to get married wearing a turban?

This disjunction illustrates the multivalent quality of the turban symbol. Older men from Punjab take it as adherence to the same traditions they grew up with in rural Punjab, not suspecting that for the young women in North America who adopt it today it has a progressive, not a conservative, meaning. For likely marriage partners on this continent, it carries the same message of gender equality, even feminism, that it does for the wearers. While many North American Sikh males celebrate this symbolism, others no doubt shy away from it. Certainly most India-born males, to whom some of the women of the family may be looking for potential spouses, are not likely to take the wearing of the turban on the part of a candidate for marriage positively.

Women described being negatively stereotyped within their own communities as either religious zealots or radical feminists—this seemingly paradoxical duality—just for wearing the *dastaar*. People at the *gurudwara* offered sympathies for their reduced chances of finding a good match in marriage because of the *dastaar*. Sometimes they might be ostracized from circles of women, only to be told that the participants imagined that because they wore a *dastaar* they were conceited or snobbish, even though they had never had any conversations with that group. Daljot recalled feeling alienated once she started wearing the *dastaar:*

> When I first started wearing it, I remember the women at the *gurudwara* were commenting on how I was religious now. And I thought to myself that I had always considered myself religious before! People have stereotypes about it, though; they think, "OK, she is wearing a *dastaar,* I'm not good enough for her or she is not going to talk to me." Some people even think that women wearing *dastaars* are snobs.

By adopting (and adapting) this symbol, Sikh women can be misinterpreted by their own communities as trying to take on masculine identities and rejecting feminine norms. Notice how Rajvinder contrasts what she considers Punjabi feminine qualities with the community's ideas about "feminists":

> A woman asserting herself is something that is really threatening in a culture that in a lot of ways molds you to be acceptable to everyone else and ignore your own needs. People say, "Oh, that's a staunch feminist! She is going to stomp all over and yell and not be sensitive and not be feminine." And I thought the Khalsa was supposed to be gender neutral. Just because you wear a *dastaar,* it doesn't mean that you are trying to be like a man or that you are emulating a man. People want to know why I wear it and what I am trying to prove. I say I wear it for the same reason any man wears it, because I am a Sikh.

Another Sikh friend notes,

> In fact, everybody agrees that a turban is essential to the Sikh faith. You will not hear a Sikh argue against that fact.[3] It's just that some believe that only men have to wear it. What I find hard to understand is, in a religion that teaches the equality of men and women, how men and women can have different standards as far as the turban is concerned. A friend told me that in books published in India in the 1800s, all the baptized women are referred to as wearing turbans. I personally have not had the chance to read any of these books, as my Punjabi is not strong enough. I'm strengthening my Punjabi so that one day I can.

---

[3] Actually, some do make that argument, as one woman does in chapter 5.

Although there have been some negative reactions to women wearing turbans, there have also been some positive reactions from the community. Amanpreet found satisfaction in being looked up to as a role model for younger Sikh girls:

> I've had younger women and girls come up to me and say they thought it was wonderful. I think it makes me more confident when they see me as a role model; that really means a lot when they tell me I am an inspiration to other people. My friend and my sister in-law (who wear *dastaars*) have both been my role models. I have always looked up to them and seen the kinds of things they do and the way they live their lives. It has always given me a lot of inspiration, and so I just think that I have this responsibility to do that for others, to be a role model for others.
>
> I think it is very important for young girls to have women role models. Barbie is so typical in our society. There is this little twelve-year-old girl I know who wanted to take *amrit*, even though no one else in her family had. And I looked at her one day and she was sewing clothes for Barbie. Barbie was wearing a miniskirt and Barbie was wearing this hairstyle. . . . I said to her, "Have you ever thought that it might be possible for Barbie to have long hair like you and dress like a traditional Sikh?" And she said, "No, that isn't possible." So I said, "Let's try putting a turban on Barbie and see what Barbie looks like." She thought it was really odd that Barbie could have a turban.

Another woman's experience put the *dastaar* solidly in the beauty camp; she had no need of a turban-Barbie to come to this conclusion:

> I had a friend tell me once that a middle-aged man from India, who was a guest in her home, had told her that her sister, who was not *amritdhari* and hence didn't wear a turban, was beautiful because she had long black hair. He then said that my friend was not beautiful because her hair was bound up in a turban. I was shocked, not only at the gall of this man for insulting his host's daughter, but also because I had never come across this before. I have had the complete opposite experience. Grown men of various ages have come up to me and told me that they love my turban. Some have said that they think my turban looks very attractive, and some have even said that I am beautiful. The interesting thing to note is that none of these men were East Indian. They were white, black, or oriental. It's true that some East Indian men think that women do not look good in turbans; that it isn't feminine. It just goes to show you how our ideas on beauty are so culturally based. Many white, black, and oriental men find the female turban beautiful, and many East Indians do not. Just something to think about.

I think that all the Sikh women who are wearing turbans are quite feminine. They are confident and full of grace, and actively enjoy being women.

The *dastaar* is not equated by these women with being less feminine/ more masculine, and it is not used as a confrontational feminist statement. Nor does it represent a simple religious or cultural conservatism, as it is often portrayed by journalists and academics intent on defining orthodox Sikhs as "fundamentalists." Rather, the female turban creates a modified feminine identity that does not completely conform to the norms of either Sikh or non-Sikh conventions or expectations. Within the local group (Sikh), there is conscious manipulation of this symbol to illustrate the religious ideals of gender equality and traditional gender roles. The *dastaar* acts as a subversive internal critique and represents a middle ground that, although not completely accepted, cannot be rejected, either, because it is based on a substantiated interpretation of religious scriptures. It embodies the values and the essential qualities of what the community considers its own identity —resistance to conformity and power, commitment to one's faith. The *dastaar* also sends messages to the larger non-Sikh community: It states that the wearer will not internalize the prevailing images of feminine body concepts (i.e., Barbie syndrome) and that she has her own priorities and a secure enough self-concept to refuse to be defined by any stereotypical category of womanhood. The female *dastaar* therefore is a private and public symbol that communicates multiple meanings (spiritual, social, political) to multiple audiences (self, Sikhs, non-Sikhs). It is a statement of a particular woman's personal identity that has been culturally negotiated, using body symbolism, to signal acceptance of a covenant of religious commitment and resistance to social pressures to conform to prevailing standards of femininity.

Role Models

The *dastaar* looms large in the minds of some younger Sikh women as a symbol of women taking back that sense of gender equality that they feel was lost after the Guru period. We see a similar symbolism attributed to the resumption of the veil among some Islamic women, an act that carries a different meaning for the Western world than it does for some of the women who choose it (Hessini 1994). In *In Search of Islamic Feminism*, Elizabeth Fernea notes that the use of the headscarf by Muslim women, perceived by many as a willingness to adhere to tradition, allows them more leeway in their actual behavior than if they had gone bareheaded (1998). The cultural capital of such symbols can be used for various ends, sometimes diametrically opposed to the prevailing meaning of the symbol itself.

Other capital drawn on by the women with whom we worked consists of the long pageant of Sikh women through history, many of whom continue to serve as inspiration. For some, familial role models are more significant. And when a young woman calls her grandmother her role model, who can accuse her of radicalism?

Karanjeet recollects,

> I didn't hear a lot about Sikh women throughout history while I was growing up, but I would say that my role model was my grand-mother. My dad laughs anytime I tell him about this, but my role model was his mother. She was a very strong woman, very pure, very disciplined. I was around seventeen when she died. I was six when we came to Canada, so I didn't see much of her after that except for when we would visit. But the stories I hear about her, how strong a person she was, that really encourages me . . . 'cause then you feel "Well, it is a part of my family"; I am proud to have her as a relative. After she died, we went to India a year later. All I heard about her was great things . . . never anything about that she didn't treat this person nicely. She was always a good person who helped others. My mom, being her daughter-in-law, never had any problems with her. So she would definitely be my role model.

Other interlocutors related to various women in Sikh history who were in familial roles with regard to the Gurus—such as wives, sisters, and daughters—and who also were nonincendiary choices in political terms:

RAJVINDER: I think I have had role models in both historical and personal ways. I think I was able to take characteristics of people I really re-spected and found that they were similar in those historic figures and my family members. I think that one thing that is definitely there is a clearly resolute sense of character.

Women of my mother's generation and older have, as a group, an extremely strong ability to put others before themselves. I guess it has just been ingrained, to do things for everyone else.

So it is that sense of family and sense of responsibility that I really respect. Being brought up here—to think about myself all of the time [laughs] and "what is good for me and what am I going to get out of this?"—I see these people who have spent all of their lives doing for everybody else and I really respect that sense of sacrifice.

I think that is the same thing that allowed Sikh women in the past, whatever century, to have that ability to really look beyond and outside themselves and to do things, in either the communities or in their own devotion, that were really out of the ordinary. I think it is that very, very strong sense of character that carries these women through, which we have lost.

I don't know, maybe as we get older, we will change too, but I see the way that older women are with their children and they are so caring and so able to just look beyond themselves. I am really hoping that all of us, myself and my friends, people of my generation, can carry that forward 'cause I think we are more self-centered and concerned about what is going on in our own little circles rather than beyond. I am really hoping we can carry that forward, but I don't see it in myself. . . . I make an effort for it, but it's one thing to consciously try and be that way and it is another thing to have it come naturally. I remember one story that has always impacted me, it's that of Guru Arjun ji and Bibi Bhani. Have you heard it?

My maternal grandfather told me this story when I was really little. Guru Arjun ji was the fifth Guru and Bibi Bhani was his daughter or daughter-in-law. He was taking a bath and doing his prayers, and she was helping him with the water. This was the Guru —to her more than any kind of family relationship—and all the stories of Bibi Bhani have reinforced that image of her, that she was a very devoted Sikh before she was anything else. Anyway, there is a stool that has four wooden legs and then has woven material in between, and one of the legs broke on the side and she didn't want the Guru to be interrupted while he was doing his prayer and meditating while he was taking his bath, so she put her foot underneath the peg so it wouldn't wobble. He noticed a while later that there was blood coming from her foot.

To me, that kind of automatic devotion and the ability to do that . . . it is a very small thing. There are women who went to war and sacrificed their sons and have done all of this, but for some reason that very little story about a very little thing really always meant a lot to me, but I can't really pinpoint why that is. Bibi Bhani just putting her foot under this thing and letting herself bleed for a while just so that she wouldn't interrupt, that is the kind of devotion I really respect. Because I'm the type of person who always thinks about myself first [laughs].

HARINDER: There is a story about Mata Khivi and how she basically initiated the concept of "*sangat* and *pangat*." *Sangat* means "everybody" and *pangat* is when you are eating together, everybody is sitting in the lines and rows and there is no distinction of what you are or who you are in terms of gender or caste system, and she is basically the one who basically brought that about and helped her husband in ensuring that. Mata Khivi would unselfishly do *seva* [would serve] for hours on end and would make sure that everyone else was taken

Figure 3.1   Painting of Mai Bhago leading Sikh warriors into battle.

care of before she would take care of her own self. I think that was
very inspirational.

Women don't grow up knowing these stories, and that is one
thing that prompted me to do a project on women in Sikhism for
school. I work with a lot of young Sikh kids and I asked them a question; these were younger children. . . . I said, "If I were to ask you to
draw me a picture of the bravest Sikh soldier, how would that soldier
look to you?" All of them said, "He would be big and tall and have a
beard and sword." And everyone, whether they were male or female,
they all said the that. Not one said "she," 'cause if you look at our
gurudwaras, you see pictures of Sikh warriors that are a majority of
men and few women. I asked them, "Why did you all say 'men'?" and
they said, "Well, that is what is up on the walls; those are all the pictures we see in the books we read." So I feel there should definitely be
more emphasis put on women.

Two historical role models mentioned most often, however, were
women warriors: Mai Bhago and Sundari.

Mai Bhago is a woman who is often pictured in Sikh literature as a grace-
ful, strong, turbaned figure astride a charging horse and leading an army into
battle (Figure 3.1). Her story takes place during the early eighteenth century,

when Guru Gobind Singh's armies were being hunted down by the Mughal rulers of Punjab. Her husband was a soldier in an army of forty who, on the eve of a terrible battle, decided they did not want to fight for their Guru any longer. They told Guru Gobind Singh they were not his Sikhs and he was not their Guru and went back to their village. When they got there and told their wives what they had done, Mai Bhago came forward and told her husband to go take care of the children and the housework because it was now up to her to go fight for her Guru. As she gathered the other women in the village to go to the battlefield, the men were so filled with shame that this woman showed more strength of character and faith, they promised to return at once. Mai Bhago led the forty Sikhs back to the battle and helped save the Guru that day. According to Sikh tradition, she was given the position of Guru Gobind Singh's personal bodyguard as a reward for her faithfulness and bravery. An important part of the image of Mai Bhago that is conveyed to women today is that in every painting or print she is in the midst of battle, leading the charge, and is represented as wearing a turban.

When asked the question "Who would be an ideal Sikh role model?" Daljot answered:

> Mai Bhago. Do you know her? She was Guru Gobind Singh's body-guard who led the forty Sikhs who said we're not your Sikhs and you're not our Guru, sort of thing. . . . She was a true picture of the saint-soldier image. She had her own family, but she went out and performed her duty for the *panth* [Sikh community]. She went out and took up arms and led a small army of Sikhs back to the Guru.

Most of the other important women in Sikh history are represented as wearing a typically feminine headscarf and are noted for their fortitude in the face of horrendous tortures by their enemies and the sacrifices they willingly make for their families. Mai Bhago, in contrast, displays the very essence of the saint-soldier image of the Khalsa. She performs her duties as wife and mother while her husband is away fighting alongside the Guru. But when her husband fails in his duties to fulfill his role, Mai Bhago thinks nothing of taking his place and rallies the other wives in her village to do the same. Is this why she is portrayed with a turban? She takes on the physical and masculine role of soldier, and so she is given the honor of wearing a *dastaar* into battle. Or perhaps the artists representing her imagined all women of her day were equal in status to their men, including the wearing of the *dastaar*. Today both of these interpretations play into the community perception of young women who choose to wear the turban; some perceive it as a gesture (however honorable) toward masculinity while others view it simply as being Sikh in terms of the gender equality promised in the religion.

Another role model who is frequently mentioned in discussions among younger diasporan women is the literary character Sundari. This character, created by the early-twentieth-century author and poet Bhai Vir Singh, strikes a deep chord in feminine Sikh identity. When the novel *Sundari* was published in 1898, Sikhs in Punjab were in a period of decline. Religious teachings had been pushed aside after the annexation of Ranjit Singh's former kingdom, and Sikh morale had hit a low point. Bhai Vir Singh had found a way to inspire courage through his first literary attempt, and it has continually reemerged to shape Sikh ethos for over one hundred years. Nikky Gurinder Kaur Singh has analyzed Bhai Vir Singh's literary texts against the feminine-orientated language of the Sikh scriptures. She feels that "Sundari is the incarnation of all that is best in Sikh life and tradition, yet she does not remain a remote paragon of excellence or a distant goddess to be worshipped on a pedestal. Physically and psychologically she embodies the power that is being articulated by the modern feminists" (1993: 203–4). Sundari is similar to Mai Bhago in that she is a woman whose faith in the Guru's teachings is everything, and this inspires her to live her life courageously and without fear.

Throughout the novel, Sundari is desired by Mughal rulers and kidnapped for her physical beauty but always manages to escape through her inner virtues of bravery, devotion to her faith, and willingness to take an active role in liberating herself and others from forces that seek to contain them. In almost every Sikh home inhabited by young women, visiting anthropologists are asked whether they have read *Sundari.* Interlocutors would talk about how much the novel had meant to them growing up. Some younger women said that Sundari was a childhood hero they had read about in religious comic books. Many connected feelings of power and bravery to imagining that they were the literary heroine Sundari:

DALJOT: I remember being in bed at night with a flashlight under my covers reading this comic book. It was about the book *Sundari.* I loved it because there were lots of comics about brave Sikh men who got to do all of these heroic things, but this was the only one I could find that had any girls as heroes. I used to jump around and pretend I was her as she rode with the Khalsa in and out of jungle battles.

JASVINDER: We used to have these comic books. They were about the Gurus, but they had some about Sundari and Satwant Kaur. They were two Sikh women who were heroines. Have you heard about them? So that was great; I started to read those and pretend "I am Sundari . . . I am Satwant Kaur . . . [laughs]!" These were just wonderful inspiring women that became so ingrained in me. Still to this day, Sundari and Satwant Kaur are truly a part of me because I read those comic books so many times. You probably had Lynda Carter, but to me Sundari and Satwant Kaur were like me.

SURJEET: I had a couple of comic books when I was small. We had comic books of all the Gurus and I had one of a woman, I think it was Bibi Sundari. The moral was her bravery and her willingness to stick to her faith. She was kidnapped on her way from her wedding to her in-laws' home. The men all got scared; they weren't protecting her and they were outnumbered by the enemies. But through her cleverness and her bravery she managed to get to help and she saved herself. She was so brave [laughing] . . . I read it over and over again! It was like "Wow, she's a girl."

This character is the only other woman besides Mai Bhago who is commonly portrayed as wearing a turban in Sikh religious and traditional art. Every cover of *Sundari* represents her as wearing a turban and riding on a charging horse. Nikky Singh summarized Sundari's relevance to Sikh theology as she observed: "Sundari is a living person, living in actual life truths and morals enjoined by the Sikh faith. She is a person in flesh and blood who gallops freely with men, cooks with them, and with them, worships the Transcendent One. She is not a sleeping beauty awaiting her prince charming" (1993:204). This archetype of a Sikh woman who is both devoted to her faith and socially independent is thus symbolically connected to the wearing of a turban. It is also noteworthy that both Mai Bhago and Sundari accept more traditional roles under normal circumstances, but when faced with choices to either renounce their faith or fight for their own or others' liberation, they do not hesitate to fight. In the context of Sikh gender roles, these two women have earned the right to wear the turban and all the symbolic meanings that go along with it. It is not surprising why young women growing up in North America would see them as indigenous role models, Sikh parallels to Lynda Carter.

Negotiating the Ideal

The attempt to conform with religious ideals about identity can lead to conflicts for some younger women. Taranjeet spoke at length about her experiences trying to construct her own identity as a Sikh. Although her experiences and conclusions may not be typical in many ways, she spoke so intimately and eloquently that this narrative deserves its own textual space here.

Like many teenagers of any culture, Taranjeet had a particularly hard time sorting out her identity as an adolescent. Mixed signals were being sent as to just what was acceptable behavior for a young Sikh woman, and her narrative provides a good example of the agency that young women use to negotiate a comfortable space within Sikh religious ideals and cultural norms (both Punjabi and Western). Taranjeet went to Sikh youth camp the summer after her parents were having marital problems and considering a divorce. Her whole world had been turned upside down in her late teens, and she connected this to her entry into Sikhism:

> I was definitely into the Americanized identity in the sense that I was way too cool for Indians [laughs]. But at this point in my life, I was really terrified and I think that it was the one time I had ever prayed in my life; it came from something very deep. I think it just came from the fact that this divorce was something completely out of my control and in trying to regain some control, I turned to religion. There was something very deep about the whole essence of the religion; it struck me it was about love, and the people who ran the camp were very loving. I said to myself, "Look at this family, they are together!" and I think I associated a close family with the religion of Sikhism because it was a unity of brotherhood and sisterhood, and there is no caste system and everyone is equal. Because of the prospect of my parents' divorce, I felt like we were going to be shunned, and I think I thought the religion would give me somewhere to turn. So I think the fact that I loved this aspect of family and I related it to the religion, this is what made me want the identity too. . . . I have never really thought about it like this before, but it was definitely linked to the whole aspect of family and love and feeling like you belonged somewhere, and I think at that time I felt that I didn't really belong anywhere.

Taranjeet linked these early attempts at establishing a Sikh identity with some really positive changes in her life. She said she had been very shy previously, but that started to change over a year or so. Her grades started to improve and she started to have close friendships with other Sikhs for the first time. She started out by not cutting her hair anymore and then moved on to not shaving her legs, as Khalsa Sikhs are prohibited from cutting any hair on the body. The issue of shaving her legs was the beginning of Taranjeet's conflicts with her mom over her embracing of a specific identity:

> I thought to myself, if I am keeping the uniform, I need to stop shaving, so I stopped and my mom was like "What the hell are you doing? You are a fanatic! The whole essence of the religion is not about keeping your hair. If you want to keep your hair that is fine, but what about all of this other stuff? Do you really know the essence of the religion?" But I felt that this was my identity, and I felt like I wasn't taking on the full identity. So this was the first time that I was going to step away and break away from what my mom or anybody else thinks. If I am going to really have this identity, then I am going to do it right.
>
> It wasn't really beautiful. I had a real problem with my hair because you can't really tell I didn't cut it. It just doesn't grow right.

And especially when you first stop shaving, it is just disgusting; it is bristly and just horrible! A lot of your ideas about beauty come from the norm . . . so the way I carried off not shaving was to just keep in people's faces, like I went around saying, "Yeah, I don't shave!" I would wear shorts on purpose because I would rather me present the idea than other people noticing or whispering, "She doesn't shave." It was totally a defense mechanism. I feel like with a guy, you know they have a turban, they have their identity and they have to deal with it, so I think it was my way of making up for not having the turban and not being able to tell that I stopped cutting my hair.

Facial hair is an issue for many Sikh women in North America, as the face is the one part of the body that is never hidden by clothing. Facial hair, unlike underarm and leg hair which *might* be acceptable in some circles of the wider society ("They don't shave in Europe, did you know that?"), is unacceptable in North American culture. Although many Sikh women feel proud to show to the world the hair that God gave them, others have gone through a long struggle to be accepting of it. When one woman heard we were writing a book about Sikh women, she came forward to tell us about how she came to grips with facial hair:

> I had taken *amrit* in my teens, before I had developed a problem with facial hair. One day, my father told me that there was an *amrit* ceremony and asked me if I wanted to participate. While I knew that someday I would take *amrit*, I wasn't ready at that point. I was only in my mid-teens. But I didn't want to disappoint him. I knew how much it would mean to my parents.
>
> I wasn't ready for a variety of reasons. But one of those reasons was that I was starting to notice that I may have a problem with facial hair. I had very fine hair all over my face. I was worried that it may grow longer. It would be much harder to deal with it if I was *amritdhari*. But I put that worry to the back of my mind, hoping that it wouldn't become a problem.
>
> Well, it became a problem. The hair was very noticeable. I didn't know how to tell my parents that it was bothering me, and I wanted to do something about it. Like a child, even though I was in my late teens, I kept expecting my parents to come to me and say, "OK, you've got a problem, and we need to take care of it." I expected them to take the initiative because after all they were my parents, and surely they should understand that as a female in our society having all this facial hair was not good for me. I kept waiting for them to do something about it.
>
> When nothing happened, I finally confronted them on it. And they said that yes, they had noticed that it was getting out of hand, and they had discussed between themselves what could be done about it, but they assumed that because I hadn't said anything to

them, it didn't bother me. So they were waiting for me to come to them.

My parents were very supportive. They knew that it wasn't going to be easy for me, because the minute I removed any of the hair, I would have broken my *amrit*. And this was a decision they couldn't make for me. It was a decision that only I could make because I'm the one living my life, not them. At the end of the day, I'm the one who will be held accountable by God for all my decisions, even those I felt I had to make to please others.

It was at this point, with this realization, that I really started the transition from child to adult. I came to realize that throughout my life, everything I had done was because in fact I had chosen to— even when I justified it by saying that my parents made me, my friends made me, or I did it because I thought so-and-so would be happy. The truth is, I chose to obey or disobey. I used my brain to make a decision and then I acted on it.

Well, I had tests done to see what the problem with my hair was, and I discovered I had a hormonal imbalance which could be controlled by medication. But the hair I already had needed to be treated permanently, and I decided to start electrolysis. I chose to break my *amrit*. I realized I had a medical condition that needed to be treated.

It's not a choice I made lightly, but it's one I've never regretted. I'm still Sikh, but I'm no longer *amritdhari*. I follow all the other principles of Sikhism, except this one. The only thing in my life that has changed is that now I am going for electrolysis. But I refuse to change the rules of the religion to make life easier for me. I consciously chose to break *amrit* to take care of this problem. The facial hair is only a symptom; I have to treat the underlying issue of the hormonal imbalance, which I am doing. Eventually I believe there will be no more new hair growth. Then I will take *amrit* again, and this time it will be for keeps, and for the right reasons. I am now keeping this goal in mind with every decision I make.

This person would in no way suggest that other young girls facing this issue should take her solution as a model. She emphasizes that she shares this story only in the interests of bringing this often hidden issue into public focus. That it is a serious and not a trivial matter in North America is illustrated by the fact that depression and even suicide have been results of peer pressure over facial hair among teens. A Web site dedicated to airing the questions and views of young Sikhs receives many e-mails from adolescent girls regarding the hair question.

Let us return to Taranjeet's account of the steps she took toward a turban-wearing-and-hair-respecting lifestyle:

I went to this camp and I met these two guys who I became friends with and I asked them, "Why is it that a girl doesn't have to wear a turban if the guys do?" One of the guys said, "You don't need the identity of a turban; it's fine." And I wanted to go along with him because that was the easier way, but I knew there was no logic in what he was saying to me. Then I met another very religious guy and I had this same conversation and he said to me, "Well, why don't girls wear turbans? Do you want me to tie one on for you?" And I was like "OK, cool, let's tie one on me!" And so he tied one on and when people started coming back after break, it was like dead silence. I was being stared at, and it was like people were just in awe that I had worn a turban.

But it was weird; I felt really overwhelmed, and after a while I felt like I couldn't take it off so I figured I would just keep it on for a week or two. Then all of these little girls started coming up to me and they would be like "Oh my god, that is so cool that you are wearing a turban! I want to wear one too!" So three little girls wound up wearing a turban and then I felt like I really couldn't take it off!

On the other hand, the minute I started wearing the turban people started looking at me like I was a strange creature, and I began to feel very alienated. So I started wearing makeup to be cool . . . like who wears lipstick at Sikh camp [laughs]? So I am wearing this turban and I am wearing lipstick . . . and the turban is this Nihang style[4] because this guy had tied it for me [everyone is laughing as she holds her hand way above her head to show us how big it was]. . . . I looked like a cone head because this turban was so big!

Taranjeet explained how kids stopped asking her to sneak out at night because she was viewed as so religious now because of the turban and how the aunties in the camp had started to spread gossip that her relationship with the guy who was tying her turban every morning was inappropriate. She felt confused because she was getting all of these compliments for wearing the turban but was being alienated from the other girls her own age at the same time. She also felt it was a double-edged sword with being praised for her commitment to Sikh ideals to her face but being branded as a "trash girl" by the aunties' gossip.

Taranjeet reflected on how she was permitted to drop some of the traditional gender rules because of this new, classically male, identity marker:

The other really interesting thing at camp was that once I put the turban on, when all the girls went down to learn the dances, I was invited to go down with the guys and do Sikh martial arts, all because I had the turban on [laughing]! . . . It was great because I

---

[4] Nihangs ("crocodiles") were a historical group of Sikh warriors who wore characteristically high turbans.

totally pinned down this guy! I was trying to pin him down and everyone was shouting, "Go! Go!" And I know he was trying to be gentle with me so I whispered to him, "You are so sexy," and he was like "What?!!" and the next thing I knew, I got him down! It was great because we had this instructor, a big American Sikh, and he never figured out how I got this guy down! So I basically hung out with the guys, and it was really interesting because I would have wanted to do this anyway. I would have never really wanted to go learn those dances. But because I had the turban on, they said, "You can be one of us, you are different, you are welcome here." And as far as getting to wrestle with the guys, I don't think any uncle would have been saying [in a Punjabi accent], "Go, go wrestle with the guys," if I hadn't worn the turban.

When Taranjeet came home from camp, she wasn't quite sure what to expect from her family and friends regarding her wearing the turban:

My parents had a big surprise party for me when I got dropped off from camp, and both of my grandmothers were there. But when I walked in there, I was afraid how receptive they all would be to it. I remember walking by this mirror and seeing my image with the turban on, and I thought "Who is this person?" My grandmother started crying when she saw me, and I didn't know whether it was out of joy or out of "What the hell have you done to yourself?" I think she said something like "You don't need to do this, why are you wearing the turban, that's not what women Sikhs do, there is no need for this." My mom and my other grandmother were both like that too, like "Why are you doing this?"

I didn't know what anyone else was thinking, I have never been stared at like that; I was like an animal in a zoo. It was a party so they were all hanging out and saying to me, "Oh my god you are wearing a turban!" And there was this one girl who was very conservative, a very typical rural Punjabi girl; she was just that typical good Punjabi girl who would never wear a turban, and she just kept staring at me, really sweet, but you could tell inside she was thinking "What are you doing?" Then the guy I liked and wanted to go out with came over, and he was very cool about it, trying to be nonchalant, but I think I knew deep down that I would never get to go out with him if I kept the turban on.

So the next day I woke up and I couldn't tie the turban [laughs] so I had my hair up on top and I put a little tie around the topknot and it looked like a big carrot, it looked really bad because I didn't know what I was doing [laughs]! . . . So I come downstairs with this carrot on my head and mom . . . [pauses and starts to laugh really hard] . . . FLIPS!! To this day, I have never seen my mom get so mad! She started yelling, "What are you doing! Go take that thing off!" and I was like "What do you mean?" and tried to play dumb saying,

"What are you talking about?" [Everyone is cracking up as she describes this scene.] And me and my mom were laughing like we are now because laughter is how we deal with things, so we are arguing but laughing because it was so ridiculous. But then all of a sudden, my mom got really serious and said, "You go up there and take that off now!" and I yelled back, "No! I am not taking it off!" And suddenly she grabbed me; I will never forget how she grabbed me and said, "We are going for a walk!"

She took me out for a walk and said to me, "Tell me why you are really doing this. Do you know why you are doing this?" I had no answers for her necessarily because it had just been a whirlwind of getting myself into this thing [laughs] and now I was going to have to be adamant and stand up for the Sikh identity, you know? But I didn't really know why I was doing this [cracking up].

My mom and I had fought when I had stopped shaving, but this was much bigger. I felt bombarded because my mom was not giving me support, the guy I really liked didn't give that support, and my dad had been very neutral about it. It's funny because my dad had just started to keep his hair and I don't think my mother had yet. Even though I was the first one in the family to start keeping their hair, it didn't seem to matter that much because there was sort of no visual recognition up to the point that I wore the turban. Yet when my brother decided to keep his hair, my dad was like "Oh, I need to keep my hair now," but it didn't seem to matter to him when I did. I know it was when his son did it and he saw his turban he thought "I can't have my hair cut and have my son in a turban." I don't mean to say that my dad wasn't genuine about his decision, because he was, but I definitely felt that there were subtle differences in his treatment of the whole thing.

The turban is not just an identity marker; it can transform one's own sense of self as well. Taranjeet talked about how she felt wearing a headscarf in comparison with a turban:

I wore a headscarf for a while and you can't move as much as when you wear a turban. In a turban you can walk with your head held high, and that is one thing I remember about wearing it—I did feel like a princess for the first time. Because I did have the turban on, I remember my head feeling really high; it reminded me of those African American women who have the turban type of thing on. I remember mixing around with it when I did have it on. I put a scarf on top of it and then I felt beautiful too, because before, I was very masculine in my turban because I had an extreme version of it. But then when I put the scarf on top of it, there was something so elegant about it and how I felt about myself.

I have this one picture of me in it and I really treasure it. It is such a snapshot of me for a second and how I felt. It doesn't look like me;

I don't necessarily relate to that part of it. Instead, it's a girl in a turban with a scarf and she looks like she can really carry herself and do whatever she needs to.

But when my mom questioned me like that and just for practical reasons, like I didn't know how to tie it to start with, I ended up not wearing it after a while. I figured I would go back to it but it just never happened. . . . When I stopped wearing it, that guy I liked wanted to go out with me then.

I never had the guts to go back to that camp again because I felt like how could I ever face those little girls again who decided to wear the turban? I was really confused and really screwed up by all of this. I had gotten really religious and I had gotten my identity and I did really well and that was good. But then I went through all of this; I mean my identity got really shook up and it was so intermingled with our community.

I got really involved in the *gurudwara* and one of the *granthis* came up to me and said, "I heard you wore a turban; we would have supported you if you had told us." And when he said that, it made me angry because I felt like "The hell you would have!" I didn't get support anywhere! And I know I didn't know enough about myself, but I felt like he said it because he knew I wasn't wearing it now and even if I had been, it would not have been for me, it would have been more to say, "Look, we can support a woman who wants to do this." I would have just been an example, not a person or an individual. I was a girl wearing a turban, but who is Taranjeet? I found this struggle between wearing lipstick and the turban such a pathetic cry, but it was also a cry of "I am still a person," 'cause once I put that turban on, I wasn't viewed as a person anymore. I didn't have an individual personality anymore, I was a representative of something else. I felt like I couldn't swear or be the person I was before. I had to be an ambassador for Sikhism, but being an ambassador for Sikhism meant that I had to follow someone else's rules. There was none of my own identity left.

So it has definitely been a conscious choice of how I decided to become a Sikh. I was like a pendulum. At first I had my hair cut like a punk rocker and almost dyed my hair purple, and then I went and got the turban. But now I feel comfortable with how I feel in the middle; it is definitely different but it has been a choice. Everything has been a choice, about the whole thing, every single thing. Now I don't go around saying that I don't shave for my religion because if I decided to tweeze my eyebrows, what does that mean? Now I would never go and say that I am religious and that I am a Sikh, so it is funny that I still identify myself as a Sikh, but it is not the same way I used to. I still feel I am but it is much more subtle.

I finally met women of my own generation who wore turbans and they didn't have the big ones, they had the normal ones [laughing]. And when I saw them I felt like "Am I supposed to go back . . .

what is my choice now? Do I really want to wear a turban again?" It has been a choice and I can admire them but a part of me is like . . . I don't know what I feel, maybe like I tried and failed or just that I didn't stand up to my mom.

When I started seeing these women with turbans and I started being involved in this Sikh group, I felt myself being angry toward them or some sort of resentment. I was intimidated by them. In fact, I went up to one of them and told her how intimidated I was of her and she just laughed and said, "What are you talking about?" I never told her it was because of her turban but that it was because of the way she carried herself, because I saw that dignity, I saw the glimpse of that picture of me; . . . I saw her taking it further than I was able to and I think that it intimidated me because I was like "Am I doing everything I can to be a Sikh?" I don't always know that I am and I think the turban was so in my face that I had to deal with it. . . . We were at a retreat where we all had to work together and I think that my whole attitude toward women in turbans changed because I saw they were just people like me. It was almost as if I had done to them what people had done to me. I went back and forth being intimidated by them and overcompensating for that by going and making a point to go talk to them. I had lots of mixed emotions about it, but there was a part of me that knew I was intimi- dated by them and it had nothing to do with them, it had to do with my own experiences and my own personal choices and asking myself if I had failed. I think to this day there has been this question of should I be . . . or is a Sikh identity about going that far?

Some of the women suggested that we read a book written by S. S. Khalra titled *Daughters of Tradition: Adolescent Sikh Girls and Their Accommoda- tion to British Society* (1980). This book was written before the recent upsurge in militancy and a separate Sikh identity, and its language is very interesting in that it makes no differentiation between Sikh and Indian or Asian. There is little separation between Sikh and Hindu ideas about gender roles, and the author regularly uses narrative excerpts taken from Hindu girls and boys as ways of making his points. The other interesting thing about the language used in this book is how often Khalra slips into using "he" when talking about identity issues: "With the passage of time they become rootless by los- ing their own identity and breaking ties with their own culture. They try their best to change themselves but their color, physical features and accent of speech remain. He feels that he does not belong to either group and he is lost. He doubts whether he has been accepted by the indigenous popula- tion" (1980:62). So even the work suggested by the young women we know not only neglected the entire idea of Sikh identity, of which the turban is a symbol, but also used male-gendered language throughout! This is, no doubt, partly the time in which the book was written, and I. J. Singh writes

Figure 3.2   Palbinder Kaur Shergill, parliamentary candidate in British Columbia.

about gender far more openly in *Sikhs and Sikhism* (1998), directed specifically at young people. But such empowering resources are few.

Projected Images

The question remains how the non-Sikh community in North America has
reacted to women who have chosen to wear the turban (Figure 3.2). Although many of the women interviewed lived within close-knit Punjabi
communities, they all were college students or had careers in largely non-
Sikh public settings. What was the general public's reaction once they had
started to wear the turban?

Most women reported no blatant discrimination by non-Sikhs after
they started to wear it. Rajvinder felt that people had responded more positively than she had imagined:

I always thought wearing the *dastaar* would be so hard [laughing].
. . . Nobody really cares! You set up psychological barriers for yourself, but when it happened Sikhs I knew were asking me about discrimination. People were really just curious, and they asked me a lot
of questions. I liked that. I was in a work environment where I was
working with mostly Caucasian middle-aged men, and I was the
really different one in the group.

For the most part, just like anything else, once people get to know
you, they really don't care; it's more about who you are. A lot of co-
workers kept asking questions and once I got to tell them about it,
they had more respect for me. I think that really helped me a lot at
work. They thought "This is someone who can make a commitment,
who has a sense of character"; that's important in a coworker.

This is unfortunately not always the case among diasporan Sikhs.
Although they live in religiously pluralistic nations, which boast about their
tolerance of diversity of religious and cultural expression, it is a risk to
appear "overly religious," especially as a member of a religious minority. In
fact, there have been numerous cases of discrimination and outright bigotry
in North America and the United Kingdom against Sikh men who wear turbans. Various court cases have been fought in order to ensure Sikhs' right to
wear turbans in, for example, the Royal Canadian Mounted Police and in
other venues. Recently, there has been a problem with turbaned Sikhs being
confused with Muslims and subjected to various levels of hostility as issues
of Middle Eastern terrorism came to grip the Western imagination. Sikh
communities themselves are frequently accused of aiding and abetting Sikh
militancy on behalf of the proposed Sikh homeland of Khalistan, and in this
context the use of the *dastaar* is sometimes taken as a social/political statement in support of radical separatism.

All of the women interviewed relating to this topic were affected by the
political movement to establish Khalistan in some way. Some women used
their professional skills to lobby for international political support, while
others directed their efforts to raising awareness of India's civil and human
rights abuses against the Sikhs in Punjab. This political motivation for the
adoption of the turban in diasporan communities has been examined but,
again, exclusively from a male perspective. Although these women did not
talk explicitly about Khalistan in our interviews, it must be noted that the
time periods for their decisions to take *amrit* all corresponded with the violent insurgency and counterinsurgency campaigns in India and also with the
rise in men taking up the turban in various immigrant communities abroad
—at least partially in solidarity with turban-wearing Sikhs in India. One
Sikh friend, confronted with this correlation, acknowledged that most North
American turbaned women now would attribute their decision to religious
sentiments, but that in her case it was clearly also for political reasons. She

wanted to show solidarity with her community here in the United States and also to strengthen her visible ties to the Sikhs in India. The turban was the most public way she could assert her Sikh identity, and it created a space for her to talk to non-Sikhs about the human rights abuses going on in the Punjab.

All the women who participated in this study had relatives in Punjab whom they visited whenever possible. Most had firsthand experiences to relate of India's efforts to eradicate Sikh militants and their supporters by whatever means possible and told of relatives being harassed—or worse—in a variety of situations. In India, *amritdhari* Sikh men have been singled out as "dangerous" by Indian authorities and, for some dozen years following the critical events of 1984, were at serious risk. All Sikhs know that *amritdhari* Sikh men are visible targets for national fears of nefarious terrorist plots in North America, too, and can become unwitting targets of anxieties surrounding "foreign terrorist" activities just through their physical appearance alone. By taking on the *dastaar* in this emotional environment, the women we spoke with identify themselves—implicitly if not explicitly—as taking an active political stand in their faith and its issues. They put themselves at risk of being targets of racist and antiforeigner fears in the general population, who have been exposed only to a one-sided account of the oppression in Punjab and its resulting revolt and separatist movement.

Lisa Suhair Majaj, a Palestinian American, wrote words that could well have come from the pen of any of our Sikh friends, with appropriate modifications:

> There are ways in which Palestinian women escape the typical
> stereotype of Arab women—exotic, sensualized, victimized—only
> to be laden with the more male-coded, or perhaps merely generic,
> images of irrational terrorists and pathetic refugees. But none of
> these images reflect the Arab women I know: my widowed Palestin-
> ian grandmother, who raised three boys and buried two girls, rais-
> ing two grandchildren as well after their mother was killed by a
> Zionist group's bomb, whose strength and independence people
> still speak of with awe; or my Lebanese aunt, a skilled nurse who
> ran a female hospital ward for years, raised four children, gracefully
> met the social requirements of her husband's busy political career,
> and now directs a center for disabled children. (Majaj 1998:90)

Connotations of exoticism and victimization evoked by Sikh women in the minds of many Westerners have now been tainted, if not eclipsed, by the image of the Sikh-as-terrorist. The women we know who have chosen to wear the turban wear it for their own reasons, but they do also wear it in defiance of that stereotype and in solidarity with their brothers, who face discrimination on the basis of it to a far greater extent. Collapsing the richness of the turban's symbolism to an equation with senseless violence is itself an act of aggression against the Sikh tradition.

> Once my brother and I were at a 7-11. We heard the clerks whispering about my brother. That was right after the Embassy bombings. "Hey, look at that guy." "You know Osama bin Laden?" "Got a bomb in your backpack?" That sort of thing. Finally I couldn't stand it anymore. I walked right up to them and I said loudly, "I dare you to say that to my face!" I leaned right over the counter at them. "Well? Go ahead!" I had a turban on, too, under my headscarf. The clerks backed off.
> They didn't know what to make of the situation.

The same woman, whose brother's turban led to the hurtful suspicions of terrorist connections, talked more personally about what her hair and her turban meant to *her* (and it had nothing to do with Osama bin Laden!):

> I love my hair. I love it because my Guru gave it to me. I love to brush it and make it shine. I love to wind it up on top of my head and tie on a nice clean turban. Maybe you think I am crazy to feel this way, but I keep my hair and my turban because I think they are beautiful and perfect; they are holy; they are precious; I love them— whether I look like the girls in magazines or not.

Cynthia said she did not think this woman was crazy at all, that it was a beautiful sentiment. She gave her Lucille Clifton's poem on hair—written by an African American in celebratory defense of hair that doesn't fit the mainstream Anglo definition of beauty, either:

Homage to My Hair

when i feel her jump up and dance
i hear the music! my God
i'm talking about my nappy hair!
she is a challenge to your hand
black man,
she is as tasty on your tongue as good greens
black man,
she can touch your mind
with her electric fingers and
the grayer she do get, good God,
the blacker she do be!

(*Lucille Clifton, 1976*)

Our Sikh friend immediately hung up this poem on the edge of her mirror.

4

Intertwining Kin

O Captain, My Captain!

Now what do I say to anyone reading this ad? Well, sarcastic Indian daughter is being constantly reminded by a wonderfully stubborn mom that she should look into settling down. According to my mother, my biological clock is ticking and I am losing market value. Sometimes I get this gnawing feeling that I am a '67 Chevy. Well, that's my mom and don't you dare disrespect her.

As my luck would have it, I haven't come across any Jat Sikh men that I would approach. Thus the ad. I am looking for someone who knows what it means to respect others, not because it's due them but because they deserve it. You have to love the outdoors because on my free time you will catch me biking or hiking or anything else that takes me outdoors. Comically ingenious people are encouraged to reply.

My ideals were molded by my parents' iron bond of "Love, Loyalty" among other things. So I would want you to be an addition to the family in all senses of the word. My parents will gain another son and not a son-in-law.

—*recent matrimonial advertisement on SikhNet Web site,*
placed by a 26-year-old law student

Relationships

"Why are you (i.e., outsiders) always so interested in our arranged marriages?" an older male Sikh friend demanded as he looked over some of the questions on our interview sheet. "It is really not as big of a deal as all of you make it out to be!" We assured him that he was right but added that an anthropological project focusing on Sikh women's lives that didn't contain at least something about current marriage practices would not be complete. He rolled his eyes but seemed satisfied with this response.

The truth was, being married for nine years to a man she has known for almost sixteen years, Stacy was curious what the term "arranged marriage" meant to the women she would be talking with. She wanted to hear about how younger and older Sikh women found their marriage partners, what their feelings were about marriage, and what might be the characteristics of a good marriage partner. Cynthia, who had been married to a Pakistani man for twelve years, had come to know what arranged marriage means for Pakistani Punjabis—all Muslims—but wondered what it meant for Punjabi Sikhs with their very different religious tradition. For many of the women with whom we spoke, ideas about gender equality and how Sikhism has shaped their lives were interwoven with their ideas on marriage and family relationships. In the group of women focused on here, six of the women were married, one woman was engaged and would be married shortly, and nine others were single, never married.

SikhNet, excerpted on previous page, is a Web page constructed "by and for professional Sikhs around the world." This Web page contains a variety of different sections dealing with religious, cultural, and political issues, and it also started a matrimonial section about a year ago that is archived and is accessible over the Internet. This database contains a wealth of information on the women's ages and the ages of the men they are seeking, whether they have ever been married before or divorced, if they practice their religion, drink, smoke, or even if they wear a turban. As has been stated previously, getting any sort of numbers on this population is extremely difficult because Sikhs are typically submerged within the larger categories of Asian or South Asian or Indian on most governmental or social science surveys. So SikhNet provided an interesting—if ad hoc—source of further information.

According to the data compiled exclusively from the ads placed by women or their families living in the United States or Canada, out of a total of 188 (62% from the U.S. and 38% from Canada), the average age of the women in the ads was 26 with a range from 18 to 44. The average age range of the men the women were looking to marry was 26 to 30 with a range of 18 to 55. Approximately 78% stated that they had never been married, 15% stated that they were divorced without children, 3% were divorced and had children, and 4% had preferred not to say in their ads. In terms of divorce, the phrase "innocently divorced—issueless marriage" was used when women did not have children resulting from the marriage and it was stated in the ad that they had been married anywhere from a few days to a few months and had ended the marriage. This means that the marriage had been arranged, the couple did not know each other well beforehand, and once they were married they had found they were incompatible beyond just getting used to one another. There is also the implication that there were no intimate relations between the couple and therefore the woman could still be considered a virgin despite having been married already.

There was also detailed information contained about the woman's religious background and her personal habits. Thirty percent stated that their spiritual values were very important to them, 54% said they were somewhat important, 5% stated that they were not important, and 11% said they would prefer not to say. In the sample, 40% described themselves as "practicing Sikhs" (defined by the ad parameters as praying every morning and evening, reading scriptures, going to *gurudwara*), 26% stated that they occasionally observed such practices, and 28% said they were not practicing Sikhs by that definition. As far as personal habits were concerned, these were also linked to religious beliefs and cultural habits.

According to these parameters, the women whose narratives appear in this book are average in age range but would fall in the minority of women who are more religiously oriented; they all could be considered practicing Sikhs by the ad's definition and found that talking about their religious beliefs was highly important to them.

When Sikh women are asked about arranged marriages, one often gets the slightly defensive response of "Well, what do you mean by 'arranged marriages'?" Sukhminder wanted to clarify the definition of "arranged marriage":

> Only because arranged marriages by definition are arranged where only the parents talk to the man and his family and there is this photograph that gets passed around and that's it. I believe that parents should be the key players in the marriage, but at the same time the woman should have some say. It's like if a friend says, "Hey, there is this guy and he is really good-looking and smart and maybe you should get to know him." I could see my parents doing that.
>
> And if that is an "arranged marriage," then I am all for it because it is just another way of meeting someone. And what if that is the perfect person?

When asked what would happen if she found someone without her parents' help, Sukhminder said she would run to her mom and tell her and it would be fine but that she would expect them to check out the man's family and background before giving their consent. She said they would prefer a boy from a Jat professional family. The question of caste designations in Sikhism seemed to come up only with some of the women in discussing marriage. Not all Sikhs, religiously minded or not, believe in identifying themselves by caste and marrying endogamously within those groups. It is a subject that illustrates conflicts between sometimes dominant Indian (i.e., Hindu) cultural practices and the basic egalitarian principles of Sikhism. Guru Nanak had wiped out caste designations to create a religion whereby all were to be viewed as equal, despite wealth, gender, and caste differences. The fact that many Sikhs still place matrimonial ads both in Indian and in North American venues that specify caste restrictions is something that frustrates many younger religious Sikhs, who understand that caste is to be no part of Sikhism.

Surjeet, single, expected to include her parents in her marriage-partner choice because it seemed too important a decision to have to make on her own. She described her parents as the two most important people in her life and felt that to not include them would be unimaginable. She compared her knowledge of arranged marriages and "love matches" as she reflected:

> I guess that love is supposed to prevail, but I have just seen so many love matches fall apart because the person is not looking at the bigger picture and jumps into things. Having an arranged marriage is practical, but I mean an arranged marriage in the sense that it is mutually arranged, not "OK, there is this boy, here is his picture, and you will see him after you are married [laughs]." That is absolutely insane!
>
> That was more like the way that my parents were married. They knew each other for about a week before the ceremony. It was quite quick. There were very few people who had come over [from India to North America] at that time and they had friends who said, "Well, this is a guy from a good family and this is a girl from a good family and it seems like a good match." And bam [laughs]! They say they were lucky it all worked out. They knew so little about each other then and were quite fortunate because there are so many chances you take.
>
> Now, I would describe the choice as a mutual arrangement process. My parents and I would keep our eyes open for "prospective others" [laughs], and then when the time comes it will be a mutual agreement that this guy comes from a good family so what do we all think?
>
> But it will definitely be something that we all have full say on.

Surjeet said that some girls her age were already starting to feel pressure from parents to look for a husband, but that her parents were more concerned with her education and career choices being rewarding for her as a person. They had told her just to let them know when she was ready to start considering the idea of marriage and they would help.

Harinder felt it would be respect for her close family that would lead her to seek her parents' help and guidance when looking for a marriage partner and also had this to say about the idea of an "arranged marriage":

> In terms of arranged marriages, I think that the first definition everybody thinks of is changing or evolving. Today's arranged marriages are different. The parents introduce you to the person; you can date for two or three years. If you like them, then that is fine; if not, then you just start over again. If I were to find somebody, I would have to make sure that my parents liked him and his family. In both ways it has to be approval, you can't just come home and say, "Yo, Mom, I am going to marry him." It doesn't work that way because they have to do a long history check of the family.
>
> I think it is important that the family be involved—I don't know why, I just do. There was a time that I didn't, but I guess now that I am getting closer to the age of getting married, I think it is important to get married into the "right" family. I have been brought up in such a close family that I wouldn't want to marry somebody who didn't have that same sense of family.

Harinder mentioned again the conflict that Punjabi culture and the Sikh religion can produce when marrying. Her beliefs about Sikhism's stand on caste directly opposed her father's views, and this was a problem when it came to marriage:

> Once you turn to Sikhism, it is flat out completely said that everybody is equal, everyone is given the name Singh or Kaur because the caste system is abolished, yet there are a lot of overlapping customs between Punjabis who have been baptized into Sikhism. One of these people is my father. . . . He will say openly to you, "Yeah, I am baptized but being brought up in Punjabi farmland, I only want you to marry a Jat." Jat is a caste distinction, and in Punjabi culture it is the highest and I feel the most bullheaded! According to my parents, I am Jat so I cannot marry anyone lower than that. It is not important to me, but out of respect for my parents I will marry someone who is Jat.

In matrimonial ads placed on SikhNet within a year's period (Oct. 6, 1997 to Oct. 5, 1998), 59 out of 188 or just over 30% of ads for Sikh women residing in the United States or Canada contained caste stipulations. The most common matches sought were among Jats (40/188—21%), followed by Ramgharias (10/188—5%) and Khatris (3/188—1%). Three of the ads (3/188—1%) contained the phrase "caste no bar," which is used to indicate that caste is not an obstacle to the match and the person has no caste preferences. The vast majority of ads (129/188—69%), however, did not state caste preferences.

Other than caste, what might be some of the qualities that these young women are looking for in a husband? Jasjit, whose brother was getting married in a few weeks after our conversation, said, now that her brother was going to be married, there was increased pressure from her family to marry, too. She described herself as getting to be on "the older scale at 25," and her family had it set in their minds that she would be next to marry. She talked about what kind of man she had in mind to marry:

> I don't just want the average guy, he has got to be more than that, you know? He has to be *amritdhari*, but beyond that I would like to be able to have a decent conversation with him. He has to be intelligent, be able to speak English. . . . Those are just the basics. I think the most important thing is that I will have to be able to have conversations with him. I love talking to people one-on-one, not on the phone. He has to be well rounded and be able to do lots of things. He has to be strong in Sikhi, but he has to enjoy other aspects of life too. He has got to stand for something; I don't care what it is, just as long he has some principles to stand on.
>
> My parents think "Oh, she is being so picky!" I guess I am being picky [laughs]. I am waiting for someone to drop out of the sky. More than likely, I will wind up meeting him through my parents.

Another woman said,

> Look, I am somebody who has a lot to offer. I don't want just anybody. Probably he would not be India-born because I just don't think that culturally we would mesh very well. I am American! And many of the Indian guys just don't really get it in terms of true equality. They still want you to make tea for them. Well, of course, I would love to make tea for my husband, but I would love it if he would reciprocate, too! Then, any spouse has to really match me religiously. We have to both want to do the same devotions in our home and to bring up our kids according to the same principles. I actually think physical attraction matters, too. So . . . maybe I am too fussy. Hey, do you know any likely candidates?

Karanjeet, Jasjit's younger sister, described the kind of man she was hoping her parents would find:

> I want him to have a good job. He should be a provider and someone who will be open enough to let me have a career, like my dad has with all of us. He should be someone who does have a turban;

that is very important to me. Not so much baptized but someone who doesn't drink alcohol or eat meat. I wouldn't want to marry someone who has cut their hair for the reason that I would see that as a deterrent in their getting baptized. It is an easier process if they have a turban already. I would like to take *amrit* by the time I got married, and if we could take it together as a couple that would be great.

Daljot, also single and in her twenties, has her own ideas about marriage and what she might be looking for in a partner:

It's funny that you ask this question because my parents have sort of been hinting about it lately, and I had this same conversation with three other people in the last twenty-four hours [laughs]! I think that everyone is sort of keeping their eye out for someone, but if I don't find anyone on my own by a certain point then I suppose I will have to let them go through with it. . . .

The most important thing to me in a partner is that I have to be able to talk to him. That is the most important thing because if I can't communicate with him then I basically might as well not marry him. The other important thing is that he has the same interests as me, in that he should be geared toward achieving the ultimate goal (of becoming a *gursikh*). That's what the religion describes that marriage is. . . . It is just two people who are working toward the same goal. So I want someone who is on the same path as me and someone I can talk to . . . and then of course there are other things. He has to have a personality [laughs], a sense of humor, and this sort of thing.

[When asked if her spouse must be *amritdhari*] He has to be; it is not a choice. I didn't even list it because I just take that for granted because if he is not then I won't marry him.

Rajvinder was getting married in three weeks when she was interviewed. Her fiancé called several times during the conversation checking on her opinion about arrangements he was making. She stated there had been some tension about the arrangements because his family had wanted to follow traditional Punjabi wedding customs and Rajvinder felt these conflicted with her religious beliefs:

I know what kind of ceremony I would want this to be. The religious part in the morning, that is what is important to me; the atmosphere at the *gurudwara* is really important.

Yet I am not the only person in these decisions. It is a family occasion and I am giving in to cultural and traditional things that personally I am not comfortable with. There were certain things that I completely disagree with and I said no to definitely. There are cer-

tain traditional ceremonies that are performed beforehand on the
guy's side and on the girl's side that are just a part of the culture.
I think that fifty percent of the time, they have their roots in Hinduism. They are practiced in Punjab and in Sikh weddings just as a
celebrational thing. I think that consciously making a choice to be
Sikh means that you are committed to not doing things that are just
pure ritual and don't make any sense.

For instance, beforehand there is traditionally a ceremony where
the women get the henna [on their hands and feet]. And they put
this stuff on you and do all of these other things. I am just not going
to be a part of that. It doesn't make sense to me. That is not my
Sikhi, it has no place in a Sikh ceremony. I was able to put my foot
down with my family because they know who I am, but I still feel
conflicted about saying this to my in-laws. It was important to me to
be true to myself and yet not be too abrasive.

I haven't given in on much [laughing and looking a little em-
barrassed]. But one problem we had was the reception. His family
wanted a big reception party; it's their only son and they really
wanted to celebrate. This was something that I didn't want or agree
with, but we are going to have one and I will be there. I started off
two years ago saying I would not come [laughs] but I have softened
on that point of view. I figured this was really important to them
and the closer the wedding has come the more I have realized it is
something that you do for other people really more than yourself. If
I had it my way, I would be looking for a *gurudwara* in Las Vegas
[laughing]!

Rajvinder had decided to take a backseat in the arrangements and let
Jarnail and his family take care of the details. When his family asked her
when her henna ceremony would be, she told them she was not having one
but that they could go ahead and have one without her. Rajvinder told me
how the traditional belief is that the darker the henna, the better one is supposed to get along with one's new mother-in-law. A good relationship
between the new bride and her mother-in-law is the key to the bride's happiness and status in a traditional Indian household. She said that in order to
get the henna on the hands dark, brides leave it on all night sitting up or
lying with their arms out hoping that the design will be really dark when the
henna is washed off. Her mother's skin reacts well to henna and the designs
are a beautiful shade of dark maroon; Rajvinder said that on her own skin
tone, which is more olive, the henna turns yellow and she has never liked it.

There were other things that she really didn't want as a part of the ceremony. In traditional Sikh weddings, there are a lot of what Rajvinder
describes as Hindu customs like having tinsel necklaces that are put onto the
bride while guests throw money at her. She told his family that there was no
way she was having this done to her, but she is worried that if people try to

Figure 4.1   A Sikh marriage ceremony.

do it anyway, there is not much she can do. They were expecting about five hundred people at the reception.

Rajvinder had decided to study about the Sikh marriage ceremony (Figure 4.1), the Anand Karj, in order to make sure that it was consistent with her beliefs. She felt it was a true reflection of what she and Jarnail had always sought in their relationship:

> I think that the Sikh concept of marriage is so beautiful. I have had the chance to compare it with other religions' marriage ceremonies and I really love it. In scriptures there is this saying that a marriage is between two bodies but forms one soul and that soul's objective is to move toward God. To me that is what a Sikh marriage is all about. It is your responsibility to marry and have a family, to be a part of the community, but your two collective identities have responsibilities to ensure the spiritual progress of yourself and your family. I read that your love for your spouse, whether you are a man or a woman, is your everyday practice or your chance to have a dry run at your devotion to God. Waheguru is such an elusive concept; you can't see it and it is so hard to define. It is so much easier to love a human being, and if you can be truly devoted and love a human being, then it strengthens your commitment to love Waheguru.

In the ceremony there are four stanzas that are read from the Guru Granth Sahib, and in each of the four there is a step of progression to the ultimate liberation or meeting with God. It is the same steps between a man and a woman in terms of becoming a couple themselves. You go through the same steps in devotion to your spouse as you do to Waheguru. . . .

I think that sometimes we have lost that sense of what marriage is about. In the Anand Karj, it is important for you to be a Sikh first before you can be married in the Sikh way.

A lot of younger people are just getting married and not being concerned about the religious vows they are taking. When you go before the Guru Granth Sahib, you bow and you circle around for a reason; you are making a open commitment to each other and God.

According to one Sikh educational organization, the Anand Karj is a function which "provides bliss, delight and tranquility because two persons, a man and a woman, join together to live a holy life of peace and happiness leading to the realization of the Almighty Lord. This way the couple jointly walk on a path which helps them to achieve the mission of human life" (Canadian Sikh Study and Teaching Society). The "circling" is the hymn that defines the ceremony and was composed by Guru Ram Das. The verses describe the progression of both the relationship between the man and the woman and also the union between the human self with the Divine.

Although arranged or semiarranged marriages are common among diasporan Sikhs, particularly those who maintain the *amritdhari* lifestyle, Rajvinder said that hers was "definitely a love match because my parents wouldn't have chosen him in a million years!" It wasn't because her parents didn't approve of him, she said, but simply because she was a very different type of person than most in her family. Because Rajvinder had "chosen to be a Sikh," her ideas about prospective spouses were different from those of the rest of the family:

The kind of traits that I would look for in a prospective spouse would be different than what my parents would find for me. At one time, it was probably not so different, but I have kind of moved away from my family. They are not practicing the faith and that makes a difference. I see certain things that are important, and we really can't see things the same way anymore. I don't blame them for that; we are just different people. Besides, I think that there is a universal phenomenon of people having to hate their son-in-law [laughs]. . . . One of the basic reasons why we decided to get married and be together was because of our progressing love for Sikhi. The thing that I have always greatly respected about him was how firm he was in his principles and his love for Sikhi.

Harmanjot had been married for a year when interviewed, and, although she and her husband knew one another beforehand, she described her marriage as "partly arranged":

> I used to go to the same *gurudwara* as him and we talked with one another a few times. Then we were engaged to each other for two years. During that time we would talk to each other on the phone and we went to dinner a few times with family present. There really wasn't any time alone with each other, so I would say it was at least fifty percent arranged. All together we probably knew each other for four years before we were finally married.
>
> I think that the child should ask the parents' consent, but it depends on the relationship that the child has with the parents. I do believe that the girl should know the person. To me it is inconceivable to have a "live-in relationship." Some of my friends live together and then get married, but for myself I could never see that happening. Even when I was living alone, I knew I could do that but I just didn't believe in it. I think the woman should know the person and be engaged for a while, go out if they can, even in a family surrounding. They should get to know one another and then get married. But I don't believe in 'arranged-arranged marriages."
>
> [When asked whether her parents had an "arranged-arranged" marriage] No, they were both in England; their families had been there for over fifty years by then. My father saw my mother while she was still in school and he liked her. His parents approached my grandparents, but it really wasn't a love match. It was kind of like love at first sight for him. I don't think she returned the feelings right away, but she had no choice [laughs]."

Another:

> In a way, it is strange how in our tradition you are thrown into bed with somebody you don't know too well. A lot of the Sikhs object to the secular Western practices, like people having sex before marriage. It is true that our religion is strictly against that. But, on the other hand, if you sleep with your boyfriend at least you have chosen him and you know him. In our case . . .
>
> Well, I think the difference is that with us, the person you make love with is really the person you will spend the rest of your life with. It's the commitment that makes the difference. The rest, it's up to the couple to work it out. Probably some couples develop a great relationship while others just kind of tolerate each other. We don't talk about this sort of thing. I just hope there are a lot of great relationships out there!

Dowry Practices

The issue of dowry in Sikh marriages is an interesting example of shifting ideas of female honor and power within the diaspora. Parminder Bhachu's work in the early 1980s showed that the practice of dowry exchange at marriage was prevalent among British Sikh communities. Increased economic independence and social mobility for Sikh women was demonstrated by the increase in and quality of items contained in Sikh dowries. Bhachu concluded that sharing of domestic labor, greater decision making, and changes in settlement patterns after marriage (from patrilocal and extended family residences to neolocal residence patterns) all stemmed from Sikh women's increased economic activity in the workforce (Bhachu 1988:235–60).

Our interlocutors denied that the dowry was an acceptable Sikh practice because it was associated with the material wealth that the dowry represented and with the woman's honor and family prestige. While it may be that the difference lay in the locations of these communities and their particular populations or the time periods of study, it is more likely that it relates to the shifting identity markers of the two groups. Although some dowries are given at Sikh marriages in the United States and Canada, this practice is less acceptable now than it was perhaps ten years ago because of the emphasis that Sikh women have placed on adhering to religious ideals of gender equality and also the undercurrent of feminist principles that guide many young Sikh women in their lives. Women may be willing to accept certain cultural practices such as arranged marriages that might seem to afford them less individual freedom, but will reject other cultural practices, such as dowry, that are not in keeping with the narrowing definition of proper Sikh practices. Such "picking and choosing" of identity markers based on the level of agency they provide has been noted for Hindu women as well (Mazumdar 1994).

Harmanjot noted that it specifically says in the Guru Granth Sahib that dowries were not to be given and followed that assertion with reasons why it was so harmful to a woman's status in the household. She said that many Punjabi Sikhs still exchange a dowry and she had been to many weddings that had dowries, but that she did not have a dowry when she got married a year ago:

> It is not just that it is specifically against Sikhi, but I think that it
> is against the human quality of women. I don't think that men or
> women should be sold out like that; marriage should not be a busi-
> ness deal. It is supposed to be about men and women sharing a life
> together equally. There should be no pressure on women or their
> families to give out money. They have already educated the girl and
> raised the girl, they have done their part. The man should do his

part and, instead of asking for and taking a dowry, he should be
looking after the girl for the rest of her life and let the parents look
after their own problems and retire happily ever after [laughs].

This was a typical reaction to the dowry question. Most women
acknowledged that the dowry is still something you will see, but not as
much in religious families anymore. It was becoming more common to have
parents help the couple with furniture or a down payment on a house rather
than the formal dowry gifts and prestations. Jasjit said that her dad has
always been outspoken about his opposition to dowries for Sikh girls for
religious and women's equality reasons, but that he has been criticized by
other more traditional families who think it is important to keep the cultural
tradition going. There was only one matrimonial ad out of 188 on SikhNet
that mentioned a dowry in any way, and it said in bold letters "**Dowry Seek-
ers Need Not Reply.**"

One *amritdhari* woman said that in her circle dowries were entirely
unheard of. Surprisingly, she expressed shock at the comments of some of
the other women. This reinforced our sense of the insularity of different
communities of Sikhs, each of which assumes its views and practices are
more universal than they in fact are. There is a lot of diversity among North
American Sikhs, but it is more likely to be outsiders than insiders who recognize the true scope of this variation. Indeed, some take mere description of
it as a form of insult.

If these women understand marriage as in some ways a religious
partnership, what guidance does Sikhism give to reach this spiritual mission? Harmanjot feels that Sikhism gives specific instructions for wives
and husbands, but that sometimes the advice given in *gurudwaras* can be
misinterpreted:

> Generally, the speakers in *gurudwaras* say that a good Sikh woman
> always obeys her husband, but they don't mean that she should be a
> doormat. I think that the way they say it, it can be taken the wrong
> way. Some people might think that it means that women should
> take all of the crap in a relationship. That is not true—they are sup-
> posed to be equal partners in a marriage. They are supposed to be
> role models, even for men and future generations.

Amanpreet and Hardev had been married a few years and were well
known in their community for their devotion to their principles. Other
young women and men who knew Amanpreet and Hardev called them the
"model Sikh couple" in that they were very open about their love and commitment to one another, their religious beliefs, and their equal status in the
marriage.

Over dinner one night Amanpreet and Hardev laughed about how their relationship is viewed by other members of their families and the community in general. Hardev said that it annoys some of the older men who watch them together that he cooks, helps with the dinner, and cleans up at family gatherings. He said he particularly enjoyed asserting this aspect in front of more traditional Sikh men because he knew that they respected him in many other areas and he thought it helped to drive the point home about his interpretations of Sikh ideals on marriage. Amanpreet had said that the women in Hardev's family were known for their strength of character and independence; she felt that he had been taught from an early age about how to treat women and so had always known this was the kind of relationship he wanted in marriage.

Amanpreet spoke of how important it has been for her own faith development to have a partner like Hardev helping her. She described their faith life as inseparable from their married life, each one nourished the other, so that they both grew richer and deeper as time went by. In the early mornings in their house, Stacy would hear them softly praying together, their two voices blending as they recited the Japji. They are active in the community, especially in youth work, and are constantly on the go with either job or community commitments.

Domestic Tensions

Surpreet also expressed admiration for her husband's faith and stressed that this has helped in her own faith development. She said that before she met her husband, she was not really looking for anyone, that she was in school and happy with the way her life was, but then she was introduced and everything changed:

> I realized that I was really looking for someone I could relate to as a friend—that was my first priority. He was introduced to my parents through a family friend who my dad had asked to keep an eye out for a *gursikh* who could keep the faith. A *gursikh* is somebody who has a turban and is basically unshaven and *amritdhari*.
>
> I think it is important for other people to know what arranged marriages are really like because that is something that Sikhs are commonly associated with like other Indians. It can be really eye-popping if you don't understand about it. Mine being arranged, I can say that it is not as bad as people say it is. It is your luck or whatever. I wouldn't say it is better than a love match, but I didn't really have any preference.

Surpreet said that she felt fortunate in her marriage because she loved her in-laws, who were in England, and that even while they visited with her and her husband they did not try to interfere like other, more typical in-laws:

> In some cases, I have seen that the mother-in-law doesn't treat the new daughter-in-law the way she would treat her own daughter. This can cause friction especially if the couple is living with the man's parents. Then there are always the kinds of problems when the couple has children and the woman wants to raise them a certain way and live a kind of lifestyle different from the in-laws who come from another country and expect the daughter-in-law to give up her career and stay at home doing more traditional duties of the woman.

When asked how marriage problems were typically handled in Sikh families, all the women said that divorce was an option in their religion but that for most women of their mother's generation and older it was a rare occurrence. They acknowledged that with people their own age divorce was becoming more frequent because there were fewer pressures or interventions from family members to stop the breakup. Jasjit attributed stress in younger marriages to the changes that have taken place in the way women and men are being raised compared to how their parents were raised:

> My mother and other women like her were raised very differently than they have raised their daughters. You see, these "rebellious" daughters have been taught that they have rights in a marriage. But you see the sons being raised the same as their fathers were over and over again. I read somewhere that in India, like other parts of the world, women raise their sons gently because if their husbands ever left them they would have to rely on their sons to take care of them. You don't want to say something to your son because he might turn on you later when you need him. He might leave his bride, but he will never leave his mother because of the way his mother has raised him as an insurance factor.

Daljot said this cultural influence of gender inequality comes in again to play a role in how marriage problems are typically handled:

> Most of the marriage problems are usually blamed on the woman, but it takes two to make a marriage go right. She will be the one to get the brunt of everything; if there is emotional or physical suffering, she will be the victim. They often just suffer in silence because they don't have anyone to typically turn to. The family just gets together and says it will be shameful if they split and people will look down on the parents for letting it happen.

Harmanjot said that if the women are brought into the marriage from India and are not "Westernized," they will not typically even tell their family members about marital problems:

> It totally depends on the family on what will happen. If that family has strong beliefs then they might come, not the first time or the second time there is trouble, but only when it has gone too far will they interfere. They usually don't try to correct the problem, though; they just think they can sit down with the couple and have discussions and different opinions. Some of them don't even want to hear what the problem is, that the man is crazy, drinks too much, and beats the woman up or whatever. They are just interested in resolving the situation and getting them back together instead of going behind the reasons for the problems or the violence. They want them back together because maybe they have children and family obligations and it is a shameful thing for a woman to go to the court and claim she was abused, so they discourage all of that.

Domestic abuse is one of the skeletons in the closet of the diasporan Punjabi community. Just as Stacy was beginning to meet her first Sikh women, she was approached by two women in their early forties who had both been through painful divorces because of domestic abuse. They pulled her aside in a very public *gurudwara* setting to share their stories in intimate detail. They both felt that it was of paramount importance that this subject be a part of the research in order to better understand the cultural dynamics behind it and were dismayed that it was still such a taboo topic that many would not even acknowledge it took place at all. When domestic violence is recognized, it is often linked to the abuse of alcohol by the men of the community—another skeleton in the closet. The drinking of alcohol is explicitly forbidden according to Sikh teachings. However, it is a common Punjabi cultural trait and this has carried over into the diaspora.[1]

Jasjit said that she has seen many families hurt because of problems from alcohol abuse by men in the family. She attributed this contradictory practice to the cultural environment of agriculturally driven Punjab:

> I think it is coming from India and because many of the men are farm laborers. Because the crop they are producing can make alcohol, it just comes down through the generations that "you do all of this hard work so you deserve a reward of alcohol afterwards." . . .

---

[1] Politicized Sikhs today often accuse the Indian government of purposely encouraging alcohol use among Sikhs as a way to disempower them. However, widespread use of alcohol was noted in the Punjab region long before the current "troubles."

The problem is that all of the problems the family has stems from the abuse of alcohol. There is no family bonding and it becomes a really significant issue. I haven't seen anyone being counseled when alcohol-related domestic abuse happens. We typically discuss it in the forum of extended family and relatives when this happens and try to talk it out. They will often say that the woman needs to be more accepting or that he should just stop drinking. The problem just quiets down but just comes back later on. . . .

One woman shared her experience with alcohol and its links to domestic violence:

In some families, there is more support. My relative who lives with us now was really abused by her husband and it went on for ten years. My mom and dad tried to help her but had said that she had to make the first move. She didn't do anything for ten years. She would come and stay for a while and then go back to him thinking that it would work again. Finally, after ten years, she went to the police and they were able to help her really get away from him.

My dad used to tell her all the time to leave, that he couldn't do anything until she called the police and she was out of the house. Once you report it to the police, then we can get you to safety. But she kept going back to him, and this happened so many times until she eventually left. She went to a shelter in the town where she was living, and then we brought her here. My relative's husband was fine when he was not drunk. But it was the alcohol—when he was drunk he was the worst person on earth.

A lot of Sikh men do drink and when they do drink, it is excessively. It is not a low, social level of drinking; if you drink, you drink heavily—there is no middle ground. I think it could be due to the pressures of living here: You have to have the bigger house or you have to work more. They were brought up that way and then they just can't stop.

All of that just kind of adds up and then just keeps building, and they wind up needing to take it out on someone and it is usually the wife. Then the wife really isn't in a position to escape that situation because she can't go to her parents' house because that would be looked down upon and people would start asking, "Why isn't she living with her husband?" The community starts to talk and the family is looked down upon, so in that situation she is just stuck and has to deal with it on her own.

The problem with going to counseling is that it is actually another way of admitting that you have a problem, and I don't think that a lot of families go for the reason that they don't want to even admit there is a problem. It is better for things to be shoved under the rug or to pretend that nothing is really going on.

It is very unusual for Sikh women to drink, however. Rajvinder says:

> It's just a cultural thing; it is just something that women don't do. It
> is very taboo in India, but now when you come to North America
> and you are in a different society, you see that women are drinking.
> It is still considered unusual and not talked about in the open. My
> father's side of the family is very progressive—they have been here
> for years and years. The girls will sit down and have a beer and it
> was very normal for us to see this when we were growing up. Yet I
> know that if I took one of my friends over to my uncle's house, they
> would be so uncomfortable watching a bunch of girls sitting on the
> couch having a few beers.
>
> I enjoy being a Punjabi person and I think that there are a lot of
> good things to the culture but, unfortunately, the negative some-
> times outweighs the good. Like how alcohol is such a big part of our
> community. It is acceptable to grow up in a household where a
> father drinks, yet that is totally against Sikhi. But you don't realize it
> because it just becomes second nature after a while that the man
> drinks but the woman doesn't because it is just unacceptable.

The women in this study said that they did not drink because it was
against Sikh teachings that anyone should drink alcohol, men or women.
They also felt it was the cause of so many problems in families that they had
no desire to drink. This is a slightly different picture than the matrimonial
ads would indicate. While many ads specifically were looking for "tee-
totaling" men, 30 out of 188 ads indicated that the woman drank (78% said
they did not drink at all and 6% did not answer).

Rajvinder hoped that the male alcohol habit would change over time as
younger women became more aware of the problem and started raising their
sons differently:

> We have to bring up our sons to understand that it [drinking and
> domestic violence] is not acceptable. We also have to teach them
> how to manage their anger and deal with their feelings and teach
> them ways of communicating and resolving conflict without becom-
> ing frustrated and resorting to violence. I think that our problem as
> a culture is that we have stereotypes of what men and women are
> supposed to be like just as any other culture has. I think that men
> just don't have those outlets to be able to deal with their frustrations
> and angers. I think it all starts with the way that you bring up your
> children.
>
> I see my grandfather and other people who are older that I know,
> who think that both of these things are totally unacceptable. They
> could never imagine beating their wife or being abusive toward
> their children. But I find that the generation in between my grand-
> father's and my own, people of my parents' age, have lost their

attachment to Sikhi. In our parents' generation, there were so many other things going on in their lives because of moving here and they just didn't have that same grounding.

There are men of my age who we are not really making much progress with either. They are not really abusive, but they are not able to manage their anger or communicate effectively and that is really unfortunate. As a community, we need to start teaching them at the same time we are empowering women to be able to stand up for themselves.

There are a few people who have started this kind of work, but there has been a lot of hesitation for cultural reasons. We are not really a people that go to outsiders for help with our problems. We have social workers and many young people are seeking professional help for personal problems, but it is still very difficult for the community to come to terms with. You would have a hard time to get most Sikh men to admit they had a problem with anything [laughs], never mind getting an outsider to help them with it!

Asian immigrant communities in general have problems with spousal abuse. Often the extended kin networks available to women in the homeland are truncated or absent in North America, leaving many women with few options. Deanna Jang reports that among Korean families, fear of deportation and potential loss of children (the INS as bogeyman) prevents many women from seeking outside help (1998). This would, of course, be less true of second-generation families. But a tradition of keeping silent about family problems may well continue. Mai Kao Thao writes plaintively, in words the Sikh community might also take to heart, "As a Hmong woman, I am expected to perfect the art of hiding the painful reality of sexual, physical, or mental abuse. These conflicts cannot be resolved with silence, only deepened and catalyzed through it" (1999:18).

On the brighter side, a woman who grew up in an entirely *amritdhari* environment—her parents having made the choice to take *amrit* in the seventies—reports that as far as she knew domestic violence was simply not a problem in her circle. Nor was alcohol abuse. Perhaps this bodes well for the future families of women and men who today are making the conscious commitment to follow the path of the Gurus.

Sikhism, then, has a pervasive influence over how these women choose and negotiate relationships within their family and marriages. They specifically look for men who fit their ideals of a *gursikh* and sometimes will not even consider someone who is not *amritdhari*. They reflect the changing dynamics in the definition of arranged marriages among younger second-generation Sikhs and other South Asian migrant communities. There is a strong tie to making the marriage a "true Sikh marriage" by cultivating the spiritual aspects of the marriage union and relating this to a Sikh's spiritual union with the Divine. Traditional marriage practices and customs such as dowries or henna ceremonies are rejected as "non-Sikh influences" that detract from or corrupt their interpretations of Sikh teachings. Throughout all of the descriptions of these different stages and influences on relationships, however, there is a continuous undercurrent of statements of gender equality that are promoted and guaranteed by Sikh religious teachings. The implication is that the more Sikh teachings are actually applied, the more equitable relationships will be for women.

Marilyn French, a major writer and theorist of the "second wave" of the North American women's movement, writes in *The War Against Women* that all major world religions are patriarchal and were founded to spread or support male supremacy (1992). However misguided such a generalization might be in terms of truly understanding what religion is, in the case of Sikhism it is outright wrong. This is why Sikh "fundamentalism" must be understood somewhat differently from other movements to return to the basics of a religious tradition. For Sikh women it appears fully possible to be both "religious zealots" and "radical feminists" at the same time, as one of our Sikh friends said. Not for them the problem of being an evangelical Christian *or* a feminist (Lundberg 1997; and see Ruth 1994). Choosing Sikhism means full devotion and full equality—as an ideal at least.

As an anthropologist of religion, Cynthia had always kept an open mind about the variety of possible conjunctions there were among faith, culture, class, and gender. Anthropology's great corrective to "isms" of all sorts is to explore different labyrinths and alternate pathways. The suspicion that a media label of "fundamentalism" has obscured a fascinating set of women opened the door for a student, Stacy, to seek out the realities behind the glib labeling. Neither of us will ever again hear "fundamentalism" without a skeptical ear, nor assume that anybody else's feminism plays out the ways ours does.

When Cynthia taught at a college in Iowa, there was a bumper sticker seen on the cars of biblical literalists that commented, "God said it. I believe it. And that's the end of it." A Sikh woman might well add a line:

> GENDER EQUALITY:
> God said it.
> I believe it.
> And that's the end of it.

We could probably all learn from the simple and unequivocal devotion to the principle of equality expressed by our Sikh friends. We know that we non-Sikhs have a long way to go to achieve a just society, too.

5

Feminism/Ethnography

"Is This Subject Interesting?"

When Cynthia decided to write her 1996 book on the Khalistani militancy, it evoked immediate interest in the Sikh community. During the years when she was conducting her research, Sikhs from all over the world incessantly queried as to when the book would be published. In manuscript form, it was read carefully by several highly placed Sikhs, in addition to the scholars who gave their own commentary and feedback. Cynthia wanted to be especially careful not to make offensive mistakes regarding the Sikh religion, and she also had serious political and security concerns, given her volatile subject matter. But everyone seemed ready to help her make it the best book on the separatist movement possible.

This manuscript was to have a different fate. When the three thematic chapters you have just read were finished, Cynthia sent them to some of the same individuals (older males central to the North American Sikh community) who had responded so helpfully to her work on Khalistanis. But this time the story was different. They seemed not to find time to look at the material. The same individuals who had poured, spellbound, over every word uttered by the Khalistani militants who had been the focus of the previous work, found the narratives of these young women insignificant. One, who had glanced at a section involving the issue of shaving or not shaving one's legs, said, "Is this subject interesting?" Clearly, to him it was not.

Puzzled, and recognizing the importance of retaining good relations with the men with whom she had worked so fruitfully before, Cynthia set up an initial discussion group in a city where many of them lived. She explored the purpose of this project and why it was of interest to her as well as to the young Sikh women who participated in it. Seeking to enlist their cooperation, she explained why non-Sikh students, who would be the likely readers of the book, would be fascinated by the issues faced by Taranjeet, Surjeet, Harmanjot, and the others.

It quickly became clear that one of the roadblocks to communicating successfully to older Sikh men the importance of gender issues in the diasporan community was the widely applauded ideal of gender equality in Sikhism.

"Our Gurus were most enlightened on the subject of women. In Sikhism there are no barriers to women. Women can do everything in our faith." This was the echoing refrain: pride in Sikhism's pioneering perspective on gender, and failure to recognize that in real life Sikhs have trouble living up to the farsighted principles of their Gurus.

"Well, yes," one man said, "we know that we have a long way to go to reach actual equality in all spheres. But the thing is that in Sikhism there are no barriers, so anything women want to achieve they can. It is up to the women to just do that. The religion doesn't stop them."

The onus was on the women. When discussion turned to domestic abuse, which everybody knows is a continuing problem of the entire Punjabi community, some of Cynthia's interlocutors said the same thing.

"Maybe our women need to learn to be more assertive, not to allow this to happen. Perhaps your book would serve this function, to raise the consciousness of Sikh women so that they realize they can assert their rights. They have all the rights as men in Sikhism, if they asserted those."

A well-intentioned and principled collection of men here, but a frustrating conversation for Cynthia. The men seemed to be incapable of recognizing that they themselves have an important role to play in the achievement of the gender equality that was the gift of the Gurus—far less that they bear any part of the blame for a situation in which devout young women struggle daily with the simplest of Khalsa prescriptions (not to pluck facial hair, not to shave legs) and face problems finding a marriage partner if they move further (donning a turban). It was as if one said that the problem of racism in North American society could be resolved if only people of color would be more assertive. After all, there are now "no barriers" to their equal rights.

Many of the younger men, however, are different, and are allies for their Panthic sisters who work to claim their status as equal partners on the Guru's path.

The Other Half of the Sky

A single male Sikh professional:

> If I think of who the most important role model in my life has been,
> it was my mother. She definitely had the biggest influence on my

being a Sikh today. Although my dad had a much stronger academic knowledge about the religion, it was my mother who would be tying my topknot every morning—even though I complained about it, even though I didn't like it, even though I didn't want to have it anymore—it was my mom who stuck with it and remained strong.

When I think of the role of Sikh women changing, I hope that that kind of strength still carries on. I think it's a very difficult time to be a Sikh woman in North America. Their parents have come from India, and although this is a society in which women are given nearly equal rights—not entirely but almost—these women are brought up in a culture that does not recognize those equalities. That has led to a lot of problems: low self-esteem, low self-confidence. When that is not handled in a very good way, it can lead to difficulties throughout their lives.

It's hard for me to go to people of my parents' age and say, "You should do this and you should do that." But I know for me personally, when I have kids, if I have a boy and a girl I will make every effort to keep Guru Nanak's message alive by treating them both completely equally. Don't give either of them rights that the other doesn't have; try to avoid the double standard. It may sound really idealistic, but for me . . . I remember seeing a scene once at a *gurudwara*, where a young man had two twins, and as he was doing his prayer he was tying his son's *dastaar*, and right after that he turned and started tying his daughter's *dastaar*. To me that was the symbol of equality. That was the symbol of Guru Nanak's message.

A male medical student, engaged to be married to a female law student, both *amritdhari* Sikhs:

When I first met my fiancée I wasn't *amritdhari*, and she was. But I perceived myself as taking *amrit* in the future, when it felt right. Since we are both *amritdhari* now, we will be able to form a stable family through our common beliefs and teach them to our children.

As for her wearing a *dastaar*, I think it shows a lot of strength on her part. For me it was so easy to maintain my identity growing up, to be widely accepted both in my community and in the wider society. For her I know that was difficult. So when I see her with a *dastaar*, I see that this person has strong faith. She is pure in her belief. You know, when you meet people initially, you don't really know what they are like. But just by being a female *amritdhari*, I know that she has had to overcome a lot of adversity. Her own family has been the least ready to accept her as a woman with a *dastaar*.

When we are on the street together, sometimes people stare at me because I look different. But a lot of times people won't come up to me to talk, while they do come up to her. Sometimes African American women have approached her, I guess because they can identify with the headgear.

In the United States, I think that women who are keeping their religious identity are becoming more widely accepted in our society. And I think that as we lose our hold on some of the cultural beliefs held by the first generation, women will become more able to explore the avenues of freedom that they have here, to express their religious identities. That's the way I see things happening here, in this country.

The male Sikhs tend to have this camaraderie with one another, where we are seen as brothers. Yet we forget about our sisters. We should extend that camaraderie to our sisters as well. If one of our sisters thinks that this is what she wants to do regarding her religious belief—to take *amrit* or to keep her hair unshorn, then as brothers it's our obligation to support her, just as we would one of our brothers. There shouldn't be any difference, and unfortunately there has been up to this point.

A recent college graduate, male, engaged to an *amritdhari* woman,

When I first met my fiancée, I had not had much interaction with *amritdhari* Sikhs, and I was not very much involved in the Sikh environment. I was kind of an outsider looking in. I felt a great deal of admiration, not only for her but for everybody in that environment. I love the Sikhi that brought us together, and I hope we can continue to grow in that.

As a Sikh man I know that a lot of times Sikh men look at Sikh women and they don't want some of the characteristics of Sikh women. Like hair. The people inside our community who are supposed to be supportive about not cutting hair, not plucking facial hair or things like that, are not always supportive. It's our duty as Sikh men to help our women, to create a positive attitude among our brothers and sisters in the community. Culture defines how women should behave, but that shouldn't be a part of a Sikh definition of what a woman is. It's going to take a lot of work, but I'd like to see things evolve from the direction of culture to the direction of faith, as far as women's roles are concerned.

A male Sikh, recently married to an *amritdhari* woman:

When I first met my wife, I was taken aback, because I hadn't seen many Sikh women who cover their heads. I was a little intimidated by it due to my lack of experience with this. I eventually came to understand her belief, why she was covering her head, but at first I was a little taken aback. I felt a bit of hesitation . . . like I wondered whether they were out to try to prove something.

As an *amritdhari* I had made a promise to walk in the Guru's path, so it was important for me that my wife should be an *amritdhari* as well. . . . The fact that a Sikh woman can cover her head, in this day and age when I think most Sikh women shy away from this and might be taunted for it, shows some inner strength, some faith in the Guru Granth Sahib and the Guru Panth. It shows a willingness to go the extra mile.

One of the struggles my wife faced was at her workplace, and the other was with her family. They were very resistant to her covering her head. . . . It helped her that I believed in her and stuck with her through it. In the United States, when we walk down the street, I feel proud . . . or not exactly proud but I feel a kind of self-respect and respect for her, that she can take what I have to take, people staring or having a hesitation to get to know you. In Canada it's easier, people are more familiar with it there.

The millennium is upon us and I think that change is going to happen over a period of many years. But the role of Sikh women is vital to the survival of the Sikh community. The reason I say that is that if you look historically at the role Sikh women have always played, they have always been the backbone of the Sikh community. They have given up their lives, and they've been the support for those men who have given up their lives. Women have been pretty much oppressed by the culture that surrounds them, though, a culture which puts the female as secondary to the male. Issues such as domestic violence, alcohol abuse, inequality in the workplace, and their own lack of self-respect . . .

Guru Nanak has given them equal status. It's not their right, it's what they are. I think in reaching out to the youth we have to send that message out not only in our words but in our actions. Committed Sikhs can make an effort to treat their spouses with respect, as well as when they have kids, to raise them with a sense of self-respect and a sense of identity. These changes will happen slowly, but they are vital to the future of the community. . . .

If we follow the path of our faith dutifully, there will be no gender discrimination.

"Balance"

So, as we prepared this manuscript for publication, we knew we had some generally supportive and interested clientele among young Sikh men, and we realized that many of the older Sikh men (and women) who had recently come from India were unlikely to resonate with this project at all. But there was another issue, and that was the question of the representativeness of the initial set of women who participated in this research. Although we had never claimed they were representative or were any sort of rigorous "sample" of young Sikh women, of course their voices would be taken as in some way indicative of a broader population. So we were interested to hear the responses of other Sikh women to what we had written.

While virtually every Sikh woman with whom we talked thought it was an excellent idea to get the voices of women out into the community, we got two strong critiques on the point of "balance." Interestingly, they came from polar opposite positions on the spectrum of Sikh devotion. The first critic felt that the perspective of women in fully *amritdhari* families was not brought out—that the women with whom we worked were not as totally "into Sikhi" as some and might give a distorted impression of what living as a Sikh woman was like. She was an ardent Khalistani, someone Cynthia had known from her previous research on Sikh separatism. The second critic came from the radically alternate perspective of secularism; she felt that our initial set of women were "fundamentalists" and not representative of all the Sikhs in North America, many of whom do cut their hair, don't carry swords, and consider their faith a matter of belief rather than ritual. She is an academic.

Before commenting further on this question of "balance," let us give these two critics a chance to explain their perspectives.

> I took *amrit* when I was just a little girl, back in Punjab. There was no question about taking or not taking it. Everyone in my family has been *amritdhari* for many generations. Maybe all the way back to the Five Beloveds!
>
> To me being a Sikh today means being a Khalistani. This is our historical moment; this is what we are called to do as Sikhs: Stand up and be counted. Fight to achieve our independent homeland.
>
> I was only a kid when our Golden Temple was attacked in 1984. Many people from our village went there, to try to do something. Everyone was totally shocked, that the Indian government would send the army against our holy site. So many people were killed there. I have a cousin who was there and he got a bullet in his arm. Later he had to have that arm amputated.
>
> Even after we came to Canada, all my family continued to work for Khalistan—especially after we started hearing about how many Sikhs were getting arrested, tortured, and executed. Refugees from that started coming over here, and each one who came told another horror story. But at my school, none of my friends knew anything about this. That's why I came to the conclusion that it was up to us Sikhs to stand up for our rights, by ourselves if we have to.
>
> I know that some of the Khalistanis have done bad things. I know that some innocent people were killed by bomb blasts and all. I heard that our fighters used to extort money from people sometimes, too. But it's not fair to call them "terrorists." They are very

brave, and they are standing up for all of us. You are American; didn't your country start out exactly like this—getting independence through a guerrilla war? Look at the Jews. They got Israel as a homeland, they fought for it, and now the Jewish faith is more secure.

In your book [referring to Cynthia's 1996 book on militancy], you write about a woman who was a militant. I doubt that I would ever have the courage to do that. I wish I did. Some of these women, I admire them so much. They are willing to sacrifice their lives. Even so, they face the usual problems—like when that woman went to a training camp, she was told to cook for the guys! It is not easy— even though our religion tells us that men and women are equal. And the thing is that if you make a fuss about gender issues, you are told that the priority now is to stand together for independence, not to air our "private" grievances or to bring dishonor to the community by hanging out our dirty laundry.

I read Cynthia Enloe in a course I took as an undergrad. She wrote a book on feminism and international politics. Cynthia Enloe says that "living as a nationalist feminist is one of the most difficult political projects in today's world" [1989:6]. I agree with that. The men use the political circumstances we are in to push women's issues to the back burner.

I say that we won't be ready to get our own state until we can live up to our religious commitment. Guru Gobind Singh made us all his sons and daughters. He didn't only make us people who would stand up for truth; he made us people who would stand up for truth side by side. It is said strong women make strong nations.[1]

Really, I have to be honest and say that in my heart I feel that every Sikh must stand up for Khalistan now. Someone who claims to be a Sikh but doesn't get involved when her Sikh brothers and sisters are suffering in Punjab—who is that? This is what I think. I believe we must keep all the five K's however difficult it may be over here, where we are "exotic." I know it is even harder for a woman than for a man. Hard to be a Khalistani, hard to be a Sikh. But God made us strong enough to do it.

The second critic, who read our preliminary manuscript:

This is really a most interesting study. It is clear that these women, growing up and getting educated over here, have a much stronger sense of choice about all this than most of their parents back in India would have. I suspect that some of the India-born Sikhs won't even

---

[1] This was said by Paula Gunn Allen, a Native American woman, in *The Sacred Hoop* (1986).

"get it" on this point regarding choice. It's a function of Western society, not South Asian.

The only thing is that you really must caution readers that in my opinion this is a nonrepresentative group of Sikh women. They are much more religious and much more into the traditional aspects of the religion than many of us. For me, all these questions about shaving or not shaving, having an arranged marriage or not having an arranged marriage, drinking or not drinking, wearing turbans and so on, have nothing to do with my life.

I am proud of being a Sikh. I have studied all about the history of my community and I know all about the heroes of the past and the contributions of the Sikhs to Indian society. But there were a lot of blemishes, too, and it's terrible that the fundamentalists today don't want to acknowledge these. Some of them do not understand what rigorous historical inquiry really is; they think it is sacrilegious to say that so-and-so was actually a polygamist or whatever. But those things are part of our past, too.

I am also very much aware of the persecution faced by the Sikhs in India in recent times, and I am actively working on human rights issues. Don't get me wrong; I believe people must have the right to wear turbans, not shave their legs, and generally carry out their faith in whatever way they believe is right. My own father wore a turban, though he was not *amritdhari*. I don't have anything against these expressions of religion, unless they are taken as a simple outward substitute for real devotion.

To me, being a Sikh means celebrating the heritage of my people and taking pride in that where appropriate—taking responsibility where appropriate, too. (Did you know that Maharaja Ranjit Singh, whom many of the Sikhs talk about as if he were God's gift to statecraft, did not treat the Kashmiris very well at all?) In terms of faith, to me being a Sikh means believing in one God and trying to get myself in tune with that Divine Spirit. I meditate on that point every day; I try to live in spiritual harmony with the universe.

When I was growing up, in the United States, I faced all the usual discriminations experienced by young girls here—you know, how you are expected not to be good at math and that sort of thing. We only went to *gurudwaras* on occasion; I always liked them but got sore sitting on the floor! You know how the men and the women sit separately in a *gurudwara*. People say that's just tradition, that it doesn't mean anything, but I don't like it. What kind of backwardness is this?

I really appreciate how the women you talked to are struggling with their faith. But frankly, if you look at relations between men and women, secular North Americans, of whatever religion, are doing much better than these fundamentalist Sikhs. Some of the things they consider big issues we have entirely put behind us in the wider American society—like the fact that hardly any women speak in *gurudwaras*. In our [professional organization], at least half the speakers are always women; nobody even thinks about this anymore. So why hang out in *gurudwaras*?

It's the same with gender roles in marriages. I believe in finding your own spouse, and I found mine myself. My parents wouldn't have dreamed of interfering in this, either! Of course, Anglo-Americans have problems with male-female relationships, too, and most of the marriages are not really egalitarian, even yet. But I think your chances are still much better with somebody who has the perspective of civil liberties and individual rights and freedoms, not with somebody who thinks of equality as only handed down by God. Look at spousal abuse among the Sikhs. It's a big problem. One social worker said far worse than in the wider community.[2] Until our *gurudwaras* are ready to tackle that, or at least admit to it, I have no interest in them.

I am sure that my words will antagonize some of the really religious Sikhs. I don't mean to offend them, and I will stand up firmly for their right to worship as they like. But I can't help getting angry when they deny the label "Sikh" to anybody but themselves. I am a Sikh, too. I am proud of being a Sikh, I am standing up for the rights of Sikhs, I draw a lot of spiritual sustenance from Sikh ideas about divinity. I read the poems in the holy book, they are really beautiful.

Nobody should have a monopoly on the Sikh identity. There is room in our religion for everybody. It should be a generous religion, open to people wearing turbans or not, people who want Khalistan or not, people who are brown or white or purple. There is no need for us to be stingy about who can or cannot be a Sikh.

Your book should have the message that Sikhism was the first religion in the world to openly proclaim that men and women are equal. And it should have the message that men and women everywhere are still trying to figure out how to do that.

Here we have two perspectives that in a sense frame the continuum of which the views of our original interlocutors form the middle. We purposely sought out women for this study who occupied that middle ground where things are not entirely clear-cut—not those who accepted turban wearing without question or reflection, nor those who rejected turban wearing without question or reflection, to cite just one axis. We wanted to talk with women who were piecing out their identities and belief systems because we thought that this group would help us best understand all the factors involved in growing up as a Sikh in North America.

The women with whom we talked do not form any sort of "sample" that would be acceptable to any self-respecting social scientist. There will

---

[2] This was a report given with regard to communities in the Toronto area.

certainly be North American Sikhs who do not find their views represented here, and, to them, we apologize. This is not a comprehensive study, but an exploration, and we are not scientists, but humanists. Working *with* women —considered a contamination in the strictly scientific understanding of social research—has benefits that we believe outweigh the detriment of less than complete representation. When one of the great women pioneers of anthropology, Ruth Benedict, first went to study the Zuni, she was advised "not to set foot in Cochiti [the pueblo where they lived]" but to stay in a nearby Hispanic village. Instead, she did go to live *with* the Zuni, at Cochiti Pueblo, and wrote in a letter to Margaret Mead, "I never do get this sense of the spiked dangerous fence that Elsie, and Dr. Boas in this case, make so much of" (Mead 1973:299). We find no fences, either, and believe that the imagining of them creates not objectivity but sterility. To be able to exchange thoughts and feelings with a few, on an intimate basis, is in our opinion more productive than to "do interviews" with a large random sample. The distance and objectification implied by the latter is what makes people want to erect those fences.

Transnationalism and Globalization

Too often culture is mistaken for religion. Faith is not about what food you eat, the clothes you wear, or the language you speak. That is culture. Just because you have brown skin, eat East Indian food, wear East Indian clothes, and speak Punjabi, does not mean you are a Sikh. It means you are a person of South Asian descent. You could be Hindu, Muslim, Christian, Buddhist, Jain, or atheist.

Religion is beyond any cultural or racial or ethnic boundaries. Many baptized Sikhs are white North Americans from Christian or Jewish family backgrounds. They may or may not eat East Indian food, wear East Indian clothes, and speak Punjabi. But they have chosen to practice Sikhism. They consider themselves to be Sikhs of European, or whatever, origin. And many brown people from India have converted to other religions or practice no faith at all. There is nothing wrong with that. We are all sentient beings, with destinies unique to each of us. We are the masters of our fates. We cannot be held responsible for the circumstances of our births. Hence I have a hard time dealing with the notion that one can be born into a religion. One can be born into a family which practices a particular religion, but one must choose if she wants a faith or not and, if so, which one.

I am not alone in thinking this way. Many young South Asian men and women I went to university with, who were born and raised in North America, are refusing to let the circumstances of

Figure 5.1   North American Sikhs celebrating a birthday.

their births dictate the direction their lives will go. Some of us have chosen to commit to religions different from those of our parents, and some have chosen to commit to no religion at all. It is our right. Many of us, myself included, have chosen to commit to the religion of our parents, not as a birthright, but as a conscious and deliberate adult decision.

My nationality is Canadian, my ethnicity is Punjabi, and my religion is Sikhism. My culture is typical of many Americans in that it is made up of practices from many different cultures. Yes, I listen to *kirtan* and do *kirtan* myself. But I also listen to techno, opera, pop, oldies, reggae, classical, Latin, bhangra, Celtic, and certain kinds of country music. And I've just recently discovered Israeli and Persian music. In our house we eat traditional Punjabi vegetarian food, but we also eat Chinese food, pasta, pizza, lasagna, veggie burgers, and fries. My mom can cook all kinds of food, and she is an *amritdhari* Sikh. We all wear traditional Punjabi clothes and we wear Western clothes, too. We speak English and Punjabi. I am also working on my French! I have friends who are Sikh, Christian, Buddhist, B'hai, Muslim, Hindu, Jewish, and atheist. They are white, black, brown, oriental, or aboriginal. And like me, they eat all kinds of food, listen to all kinds of music, and so on (Figure 5.1).

Does this mean I'm not a Sikh because I'm a very multicultural person? Of course not. Culture is dynamic; it changes all the time.

My faith is constant in my life. It provides me with the principles that I apply to my daily life. If a cultural practice violates those principles, I won't practice it. For example, Sikhism doesn't believe in racism or in gender discrimination. These are unfortunately part of mainstream North American culture, but I won't practice them because they violate the principles of my faith.

   I find Sikhism so liberating. It's totally in tune with the most enlightened thinking. Some people who are culturally traditional in our community accuse me of becoming too Westernized. I laugh and point out that I've become too Sikh! And I wouldn't want it any other way.

This narrative makes clear that what we have now are not "immigrant communities" pictured as ghettos within the broader society but, in fact, "transmigrants" who are part of global society with its crisscrossing affiliations and identities. I'm a Canadian/I'm Punjabi/I'm an English speaker/ I'm a listener of Latin music/I'm a Sikh—these are the sorts of identities anthropologists face in their efforts to understand what "culture" is today. Long gone are the days when we could think of easily definable and separable "tribes" or "peoples" whose location, or even locations, could be colored on a map. Ethnography in such circumstances becomes different, too; there is no "field" to go to that is defined geographically, but "the field" is a special kind of space within the interstices of our global society. Arjun Appadurai calls these "ethnospaces" (1991; see also Gupta and Ferguson 1992; Schiller, Basch, and Blanc 1995, for the pioneering articles in this area). It takes a different kind of anthropologist to recognize, explore, and theorize this new kind of field. Trying to apply the old models simply does not work.

   The subject of transnational Sikh identity, for example, is a highly contested topic within Western and Sikh intellectual communities. There are some members of the Western academe who are reviled by Khalsa Sikhs for their deconstruction of the Sikh identity as it has evolved over the centuries. Today, although the diversity in the tradition these scholars emphasize is still present, Sikhs in countries like Canada and the United States find that the acceptance of a single collective identity and the minimizing of diversity within that identity are avenues to increased access to power (see Papanek 1994; Leonard 1989).

   The multiculturalism movement in North American identity politics in the 1980s and 1990s collided with communal politics in Punjab to form a particular historical moment in which expatriate Sikhs developed an unprecedented sense of unity and solidarity (Dusenberry 1995). Previously, Sikhs in North America were far less aware of their differences from Hindus, Muslims, and other communities of South Asian background. Before 1984, many Sikhs would attend all-India functions without second thought and would identify themselves as "Indians" (U.S.) or "East Indians" (Canada). But after the assassination of Prime Minister Indira Gandhi by two Sikhs in 1984, many found their Indian friends no longer ready to socialize. As the agitation for Khalistan on the part of Sikhs increased after that, the separation of the Sikhs from others of South Asian background intensified. At the same time, rewards were to be had in North America if one were part of a "minority group" with a definable identity. Today, "Sikh" is a known and recognized ethno-religious category in the parts of North America where Sikhs reside. Indeed, although scorned on one level (racism, fear of fundamentalism, fear of terrorism), they are seen as one of the Asian "model minorities" on another (economics, education). Because they occupy a space so oddly "betwixt and between," it is not surprising that many Sikhs want to keep at least one foot firmly on the foundation of their own community.

Lisa Majaj, a Palestinian American, writes of her household:

> Holidays became arenas for suppressed cultural battles, as my father insisted that my mother prepare time-consuming pots of rolled grape leaves and stuffed squash in addition to the turkey and mashed potatoes, sweet potatoes, and cranberry sauce; or that she dispense with the bread stuffing and substitute an Arabic filling of rice, lamb meat, and pine nuts. (Majaj 1998:87)

Such are the struggles over cultural heritage and ethnic identity, played out in the kitchens of transmigrant women. Indeed, women have been critical to the continuing definition of identity among such groups. Hanna Papanek rightly notes that "ideals of womanhood are propagated as indispensable to the attainment of the ideal society" (1994:42–46). These ideals can apply to a woman's personal behavior, clothing, sexual and partner choices, and reproduction. As women are often given the symbolic role of being carriers of culture and tradition, the result is that a group's identity is directly tied to control of women's bodies and actions as a way to maintain that identity. Nir Yuval Davis asks, "How are identities represented in and through the culture . . . and who or what politically represents women and speaks on their behalf?" (1994:414–15; and see Paur 1995).

Sikh women's conscious maneuvering within their multilayered identities has certainly been shaped by both local (North American) and global (Indian) forces. The tightening definition of who is a "true believer" is now a function of both white racism and exclusion (and, increasingly, outright violence) in the West and of Hindu hegemony and Indian governmental rights abuses in India. It is notable in the Sikh case that this tightening of identity is leading—paradoxically in most people's eyes—to a window of opportunity for women to reclaim the gender equality that formed part of original Sikhism. Although Valentine Moghadam had observed that "where group identity increases in importance, the result is women are controlled and fem-

Figure 5.2   A Sikh woman in the making.

inism is suspect" (1994:5; and see Okin 1997), this is not entirely applicable to the Sikh case. "What would you do if your daughter started wearing a turban?" Cynthia asked a male community leader. He thought about it. "Well," he said, "I guess I couldn't complain." The reconciliation of Sikh principle with male preference. For the devout, Sikh principle will have to win out—to the benefit of women. It is future generations of Sikh women who will gain most from this (Figure 5.2).

The fact is that Sikhism, despite being deserving of the status of "world" religion due to its number of believers (approximately as many as followers of Judaism), is relatively unknown. That is why scholars make generalizations about religion and women's status that do not accommodate the realities of Sikhism. We agree with Debra Kaufman, who urges feminists to recognize that religious belief may not be automatically patriarchal and limiting to women's freedoms, and that religion can in fact be a valuable resource in shaping strong female identities (1994). Within Sikhism, there is room for both gender equality and committed spirituality, and the pursuit of these need not destroy, but can enhance, community strength and solidarity.

Is a Feminist Anthropology Possible?

Marilyn Strathern and Judith Stacey are two scholars who have cast strong doubts on the possibility of the real integration of anthropology and feminism (Strathern 1987; Stacey 1991). The anthropological project cannot avoid "speaking for" others, as anthropologists attempt to understand, describe, and interpret alien cultural traditions. A key impetus for feminism, on the other hand, has been that women, society's longstanding "other," must no longer be "spoken for" but must have their own voices. If you collapse Western/non-Western and male/not-male here to the simple axis of powerful/powerless, these paths become contradictory. Can people in advantaged positions *ever* appropriately and effectively study the disadvantaged? Can they ever record and interpret their voices without co-opting them?

The Native American activist Vine Deloria Jr. is one of the most vocal, even flamboyant, challengers to traditional anthropology's habit of speaking on behalf of others. From the viewpoint of the discipline this was the height of liberal and progressive tendencies—most other social sciences not paying any attention at all to the foragers, nomads, and peasants of the world. As the people we studied became educated, many of them rebelled at how anthropologists had portrayed them, and for what reasons. Deloria wrote, of anthropologists:

> Their concern is not the ultimate policy that will affect the Indian
> people, but merely the creation of new slogans and doctrines by
> which they can climb the university totem pole. Reduction of people
> to ciphers for purposes of observation appears to be inconsequential
> to the anthropologist when compared with the immediate benefits
> he can derive, the production of further prestige, and the chance to
> appear as the high priest of American society, orienting and manip-
> ulating to his heart's desire. (Deloria 1970:98–99)

Anthropologists today can say with some pride that this kind of criticism has been taken as a serious challenge (see, for example, Said 1989). During the eighties and nineties, many ethnographers experimented with forms of research and writing that, first of all, did not pretend that the anthropologist had some sort of privileged, bird's-eye view but acknowledged his or her presence in and impact on the field situation; and, second, that incorporated the direct voices of "native" research participants, no longer reduced to the status of "objects of study" but considered partners of sorts. This vast new literature has its critics—among them those who say that books emphasizing the anthropologist him- or herself amount to disciplinary navel gazing, and those who accuse dialogue-based works as being nonetheless in the strong editorial hand of the power-wielding anthropologist.

In this project, we found ourselves in the fortunate situation of working with a group of people (North American Sikh women) who themselves really wanted this sort of a book to come out and, furthermore, understood what academia was all about and what it meant to participate in "research." They, rather than we, guided our conversations. These are not at all the circumstances faced by the anthropologist who studies, say, indigenous dwellers of a rain forest somewhere. The challenges that anthropologist faces in terms of the ethics and politics of engagement are much more complex. We were also very lucky to find that enough interest was generated by this project to provoke other women to speak up and to want to comment on our manuscript, and that a group of young men were inspired to make their own tape of interviews in the interests of helping out. People sent photos from all over. So in this case, there is no conflict between ourselves and our research participants. We were able to meet on grounds of relative equality and common interest—particularly Stacy, who is of the same generation as our interlocutors.

Anthropology has as one of its foundational myths the male adventure story—Napoleon Chagnon among those "fierce" Yạnamamö, cowboy archaeologists, impossibly high spiked fences at Cochiti Pueblo—and this prompts certain expectations of what field research should be like. (No wonder Stacy doubted that this was "really" doing ethnography!) Even many undergraduates sense that there is something of the heroic quest about the anthropological endeavor; indeed, that feature is what attracts many of them (Dubois 1995). Doing ethnography with polite young women in North America's suburbs certainly can't compare, in the prestige ladder of fieldwork, with toughing it out in the Sahara. But as someone who has visited mujahideen training camps in the Himalayas and done interviews with Kalishnikov-wielding militants, Cynthia knows that the heroic stance is not what is required. It could be, in fact, fatal. Gentility, mutual respect, and shared vulnerability are what made even this kind of "macho" fieldwork possible. In fact, women anthropologists are at the forefront of the ethnographic study of violence, succeeding in war zones, guerrilla hideouts, and brutal prisons where many men would not dare to go. And this is not because these women are hypermasculine, but the opposite: because they don't adopt a posture that is inherently challenging, provocative, and denunciatory.[3]

We believe that feminist spirituality, feminist anthropology, and feminist education are all not only possible but required. In fact, feminism in our

---

[3] That such women are frequently accused of being naive or foolish, or even of being personally titillated by guys with guns, is a function of the sexism of *our* society. When men do it, it's courageous and pioneering research.

minds equates virtually with humanism, what had gone before being a sort of half-humanism based on just half of the human experience and perspective. To add the feminine is to encounter the whole. To Strathern's and Stacey's arguments, we don't have a full response. We all continue to struggle with how to learn about others without disempowering them, how to write honestly without offending them, how to teach carefully without preempting their voices. Above all, we believe in the power of speaking, agreeing with Audre Lorde that it is not difference which immobilizes but silence (1984).

> . . . The fear of exposure, the fear that one's deepest emotions and innermost thoughts will be dismissed as mere nonsense, felt by so many young girls keeping diaries, holding and hiding speech, seems to me now one of the barriers that women have always needed and still need to destroy so that we are no longer pushed into secrecy or silence.
>
> . . . from silence into speech is for the oppressed, the colonized, the exploited, and those who stand and struggle side by side a gesture of defiance that heals, that makes new life and new growth possible. It is that act of speech, of "talking back," that is no mere gesture of empty words, that is the expression of our movement of object to subject—the liberated voice. (bell hooks 1999)

On Writing and Teaching, Friendship, and Anthropology

There are many pretensions in academia, which we chose not to assume here as we worked toward bringing Sikh voices into public dialogue. Honest ethnography calls for a certain transparency if it is to be more than "a conjuring trick" (Katz 1996). One can produce a more clear-cut narrative by using a single authorial voice, but at what cost? The reality is more muddled.

We've all been taught by the adversarial system of academics to make clear and strong "arguments" that can be "defended"—to marshall evidence that will "prove one's case" against all comers. Indeed, women writers daring to write with greater honesty and humility risk being accused of simply lacking self-confidence or of not measuring up to the highly combative standards of academic debate. Ruth Behar writes that "anxiety of authorship is the legacy of our terror at having to become (honorary) males" (1995:17). Many of us have indeed learned to behave as men in the academic arena; that's how we got Ph.D.'s and tenured jobs at major universities. But our students, a more empowered generation, won't let us get away with these pretensions much longer.

Nothing exemplifies these artificialities more than traditions of academic writing that make it inaccessible to all but the initiated. These traditions exacerbate the self-other distance between teachers and students, and between researchers and the people they study (Birth 1990). We have tried to communicate here without over-reliance on jargon. We find that ordinary English words suffice for most concepts and descriptions. We urge students reading this book not to rely on high-flown language to establish academic credibility. Credibility comes from real knowledge, of real people—not only of books. Correspondingly, the most effective form of pedagogy is an honest apprenticeship: getting students out of classrooms, where things tend to look neater, into the mess of human relations and our humble efforts to make sense of them—what Jayati Lal calls "pedagogical praxis" (1996:205).

There is nothing like getting to know a person in "the field," which is not a place but a state of mind, really, in which openness to others is the foundation upon which every action is based. Welcoming the beauty of this otherness, absorbing it like a sponge, and reveling in the joy of one's own expanded horizons that results are at the heart of the experience of field-work. Many of us are addicted to that fieldwork high, that sustains us through drudgeries of statistical analysis, tracking down of sources, and revisions of manuscripts. Experiencing this together (Cynthia talking here, the teacher gets the last word!), we developed a friendship of our own. What's it like to get to know another person via encounters with turbans, marital Internet ads, Sikh scriptures, and the skepticism of the occasional gray-bearded elder? It's a very special experience. When coauthoring a book, fates are linked for the long term; "Mahmood and Brady" now joined. For me, this is why I went into teaching. Seeing young Sikh women and men, animatedly discussing our manuscript over cups of Indian tea with English and Punjabi delightfully intermingled, is why I went into anthropology.

We urge you, readers, to think about this book in the spirit of reflexivity. Take to your heart the Guru's gift: a humankind divided into complementary halves that need each other to be truly whole.

Glossary

amrit   sacred nectar

amritdhari   Sikh who has taken *amrit*, that is, been "baptized" into the Khalsa

chai   Indian tea

chappati   Indian flat bread

dastaar   turban

granthi   scripture-reader in Sikhism, sometimes glossed as "priest"

gursikh   a true or orthodox Sikh

Guru   refers to any one of the ten historical Gurus; to the holy book (Guru Granth Sahib); to God (*Waheguru*)

gurudwara   "gateway to the Guru," or house of worship

kacha (kachera)   one of the five K's, the traditional undershorts

kakkar   K, refers to the five signs of the Khalsa Sikh, all beginning with K

kanga   one of the five K's, the comb

kara   one of the five K's, the wristband

kes   one of the five K's, unshorn hair

keski   the word for turban used by those who believe it to be the fifth K

Khalsa   the siblinghood of baptized Sikhs created by Guru Gobind Singh

kirpan   one of the five K's, the sword

kirtan   Sikh religious music

langar   community kitchen

pangat   sitting together to eat

panth   the entire Sikh community

prashad   consecrated food offered at houses of worship

sangat   congregation

sant-sipahi   "saint-soldier," the ideal Sikh warrior

seva   service

Sikhi   the Sikh way; the quality of being Sikh; Sikhdom

Waheguru   Great Guru, or God

References

Abu-Lughod, Lila. 1993. *Writing Women's Worlds: Bedouin Stories*. Berkeley: University of California.

American Anthropological Association. 1998. "Code of Ethics of the American Anthropological Association. *Anthropology Newsletter,* September.

Appadurai, Arjun. 1991. "Global Ethnospaces: Notes and Queries for a Transnational Anthropology." In *Recapturing Anthropology*. Edited by Richard Fox. Santa Fe, N. Mex.: School of American Research.

Baldwin, Shauna Singh. 1996. *English Lessons and Other Stories*. Fredericton, N. B. Canada: Goose Lane.

Barnes, Virginia Lee, and Janice Boddy. 1994. *Aman: The Story of a Somali Girl*. New York: Vintage Books.

Basu, Amrita. 1995. "Feminism Inverted: The Gendered Imagery and the Real Women of Hindu Nationalism." In *Women and Right Wing Movements: Indian Experiences*. Edited by Tanika Sarkar and Urvashi Butalia. London: Zed Books.

Behar, Ruth. 1993. *Translated Woman: Crossing the Border with Esperanza's Story*. Boston: Beacon.

Behar, Ruth. 1995. "Introduction." In *Women Writing Culture*. Edited by Ruth Behar and Deborah A. Gordon. Berkeley: University of California.

Bhachu, Parminder. 1988. "Apni Marzi Kardhi (I Do As I Please): Home and Work: Sikh Women in Britain." In *Enterprising Women: Home Work and Culture Among Minorities in Britain*. Edited by Sallie Westwood and Parminder Bhachu. London: Tavistock.

Birth, Kevin. 1990. "Reading and the Righting of Writing Ethnographies." *American Ethnologist* 17:549–57.

Bourgois, Philippe. 1995. *In Search of Respect: Selling Crack in El Barrio*. London: Cambridge University.

Bulbeck, Chilla. 1998. *Re-Orienting Western Feminism: Women's Diversity in a Postcolonial World*. London: Cambridge University.

Canadian Sikh Study and Teaching Society. n.d. *Anand Karj: Marriage Ceremony of the Sikhs*. Vancouver: Canadian Sikh Study and Teaching Society.

Carrithers, Michael. 1990. "Is Anthropology Art or Science?" *Current Anthropology,* June.

Clifford, James. 1983. "On Ethnographic Authority." *Representations* 1(2): 118–46.

Cole, Owen W., and Piara Singh. 1993. *Sikhism and Christianity: A Comparative Study.* New York: St. Martin's.

D'Andrade, Roy. 1995. "Moral Models in Anthropology." *Current Anthropologist* 36(3): 399–408.

Davis, Nir Yuval. 1994. "Identity Politics and Women's Identity." In *Identity Politics and Women: Cultural Reassertions and Feminisms in International Perspective.* Edited by Valentine M. Moghadam. Boulder, Colo.: Westview.

Deloria, Vine Jr. 1970. *Custer Died for Your Sins: An Indian Manifesto.* New York: Avon.

Dubois, Laurent. 1995. "'Man's Darkest Hours:' Maleness, Travel, and Anthropology." In *Women Writing Culture.* Edited by Ruth Behar and Deborah A. Gordon. Berkeley: University of California.

Dusenberry, Verne. 1995. "A Sikh Diaspora? Contested Identities and Constructed Realities." In *Nation and Migration: The Politics of Space in the South Asian Diaspora.* Edited by Peter van der Veer. Philadelphia: University of Pennsylvania.

Enloe, Cynthia. 1989. *Bananas, Beaches, and Bases: Making Feminist Sense of International Politics.* Berkeley: University of California.

Fernea, Elizabeth Warnock. 1998. *In Search of Islamic Feminism: One Woman's Global Journey.* New York: Doubleday.

French, Marilyn. 1992. *The War Against Women.* New York: Simon and Schuster.

Gupta, Akhil, and James Ferguson. 1992. "Beyond Culture: Space, Identity and the Politics of Difference." *Cultural Anthropology* 7(1): 6–23.

Harding, Sandra. 1991. *Whose Science? Whose Knowledge?: Thinking from Women's Lives.* Ithaca, N.Y.: Cornell University.

Helie-Lucas, Marie-Aimee. 1994. "The Preferential Symbol for Islamic Identity: Women in Muslim Personal Law." In *Identity Politics and Women: Cultural Reassertions and Feminism in International Perspectives.* Edited by Valentine M. Moghadam. Boulder, Colo.: Westview.

Hessini, Lelia. 1994. "Wearing the Hijab: Choice and Identity." *Reconstructing Gender in the Middle East: Tradition, Identity, and Power.* Edited by Fatma Muge Gocek and Shiva Balaghi. New York: Columbia University.

hooks, bell. 1999. "Talking Back." In *Women: Images and Realities,* Second Edition. Edited by Amy Kesselman, Lily R. McNair, and Nancy Schniedewind. Mountain View, Calif.: Mayfield.

Jang, Deanna L. 1998. "Asian Immigrant Women Fight Domestic Violence." In *Women's Lives: Multicultural Perspectives.* Edited by Gwyn Kirk and Margo Okazawa-Rey. Mountain View, Calif.: Mayfield.

Katz, Cindi. 1996. "The Expeditions of Conjurers: Ethnography, Power, and Pretense." In *Feminist Dilemmas in Fieldwork.* Edited by Diane L. Wolf. Boulder, Colo.: Westview.

Kaufman, Debra Renee. 1994. "Paradoxical Politics: Gender Politics Among Newly Orthodox Jewish Women in the United States." In *Identity Politics and Women: Cultural Reassertions and Feminism in International Perspective.* Edited by Valentine M. Moghadam. Boulder, Colo.: Westview.

Kaur, Surjit. 1996. "The Place of Women in Sikhism: Unequal Partners?" *The Sikh Review,* April.

Khalra, S. S. 1980. *Daughters of Tradition: Adolescent Sikh Girls and Their Accommodation to British Society*. Birmingham, Ala.: Diana Balbir Publications.

Lal, Jayati. 1996. "Situating Locations: The Politics of Self, Identity and the 'Other' in Living and Writing the Text." In *Feminist Dilemmas in Fieldwork*. Edited by Diane L. Wolf. Boulder, Colo.: Westview.

Leonard, Karen. 1989. "Pioneer Voices from California: Reflections on Race, Religion and Ethnicity." In *The Sikh Diaspora: Migration and the Experience Outside of Punjab*. Edited by N. Gerald Barrier and Verne Dusenberry. Columbia, Mo.: South Asia Publications.

Lorde, Audre. 1984. *Sister Outsider: Essays and Speeches by Audre Lorde*. New York: Crossing Press.

Lundberg, Lynne. 1997. "False Eyelashes and the Word of God: Speaking as an Evangelical Woman." In *Courage of Conviction: Women's Words, Women's Wisdom*." Edited by Linda A. M. Perry and Patricia Geist. Mountain View, Calif.: Mayfield.

Madan, T. N. 1991. "The Double-Edged Sword: Fundamentalism and the Sikh Religious Tradition." In *Fundamentalisms Observed*. Edited by Martin E. Marty and R. Scott Appleby. Chicago: University of Chicago.

Mahmood, Cynthia Keppley. 1993. "Rethinking Indian Communalism: Culture and Counter-Culture." *Asian Survey* 7(3): 722–37.

Mahmood, Cynthia Keppley. 1996. *Fighting for Faith and Nation: Dialogues with Sikh Militants*. Philadelphia: University of Pennsylvania.

Majaj, Lisa Suhair. 1998. "Boundaries: Arab American." In *Women's Lives: Multicultural Perspectives*. Edited by Gwyn Kirk and Margo Okazawa-Rey. Mountain View, Calif.: Mayfield.

Mansukhani, G. S. 1977. *Introduction to Sikhism*. New Delhi: Hemkunt.

Mazumdar, Sucheta. 1994. "Moving Away from Secular Vision? Women, Nation and the Cultural Construction of Hindu India." In *Identity Politics and Women: Cultural Reassertions and Feminism in International Perspective*. Edited by Valentine M. Moghadam. Boulder, Colo.: Westview.

Marcus, George, and Michael Fisher, eds. 1986. *Anthropology as Cultural Critique: An Experimental Moment in the Human Sciences*. Chicago: University of Chicago Press.

Mead, Margaret. 1973. *An Anthropologist at Work: The Writings of Ruth Benedict*. New York: Avon Books.

Merrill, Christi Ann. 1991. "Symbolism of the Turban: Cultural Change in Rajasthan." *The World and I* 6(2): 22–31.

McLeod, W. H. 1989. *Who Is a Sikh? The Problem of Sikh Identity*. Oxford: Clarendon.

Minh-ha, Trinh. 1989. *Woman Native Other*. Bloomington: Indiana University.

Moghadam, Valentine M. 1994. "Introduction." In *Identity Politics and Women: Cultural Reassertions and Feminism in International Perspective*. Edited by Valentine M. Moghadam. Boulder, Colo.: Westview.

Oberoi, Harjot. 1994. *The Construction of Religious Boundaries: Culture, Identity and Diversity in the Sikh Tradition*. Chicago: University of Chicago.

Okin, Susan Moller. 1997. "Is Multiculturalism Bad for Women?" *Boston Review*, October/November.

Papanek, Hanna. 1994. "Ideal Women and Ideal Society: Control and Autonomy in the Construction of Identity." In *Identity Politics and Women: Cultural Reassertions and Feminism in International Perspective.* Edited by Valentine M. Moghadam. Boulder, Colo.: Westview.

Paur, Jasbir. 1995. "Resituating Discourses of 'Whiteness' and 'Asianness' in Northern England." *Socialist Review,* Winter.

Ruth, Sheila. 1994. *Take Back the Light: A Feminist Reclamation of Spirituality and Religion.* Lanham, Maryland: Rowman and Littlefield.

Said, Edward. 1989. "Representing the Colonized: Anthropology's Interlocutors." *Critical Inquiry* 15: 205–25.

Scheper-Hughes, Nancy. 1992. *Death Without Weeping: The Violence of Everyday Life in Brazil.* Berkeley: University of California.

Scheper-Hughes, Nancy. 1995. "The Primacy of the Ethical: Toward a Militant Anthropology." *Current Anthropology* 36(3): 409–20.

Schiller, Nina Glick, Linda Basch, and Cristina Szanton Blanc. 1995. "From Immigrant to Transmigrant: Theorizing Transnational Migration." *Anthropological Quarterly* 68(1): 48–63.

Sidhu, G. S. 1977. *The Sikh Woman.* Kent, U.K.: The Sikh Missionary Society.

Singh, I. J. 1998. *Sikhs and Sikhism: A View with a Bias.* Guelph, Ont.: Centennial Foundation.

Singh, Nikky Gurinder Kaur. 1993. *The Feminine Principle in the Sikh Vision of the Transcendent.* London: Cambridge University.

Singh, Nikky Gurinder Kaur. 1995. *The Name of My Beloved.* San Francisco: Harper.

Shostak, Marjorie. 1981. *Nisa: The Life and Words of a !Kung Woman.* New York: Random House.

Stacey, Judith. 1991. "Can There Be a Feminist Ethnography?" In *Women's Words: The Feminist Practice of Oral History.* Edited by S. B. Gluck and D. Patai. New York: Routledge.

Strathern, Marilyn. 1987. "An Awkward Relationship: The Case of Feminism and Anthropology." *Signs* 12(2): 276–281.

Thao, Mai Kao. 1999. "Sins of Silence." In *Women: Images and Realities,* Second Edition. Edited by Amy Kesselman, Lily R. McNair, and Nancy Schniedewind. Mountain View, Calif.: Mayfield.

Turner, Edith. 1987. *The Spirit and the Drum: A Memoir of Africa.* Tucson: University of Arizona.

Index